The CREATIVE *Landscape of* AGING

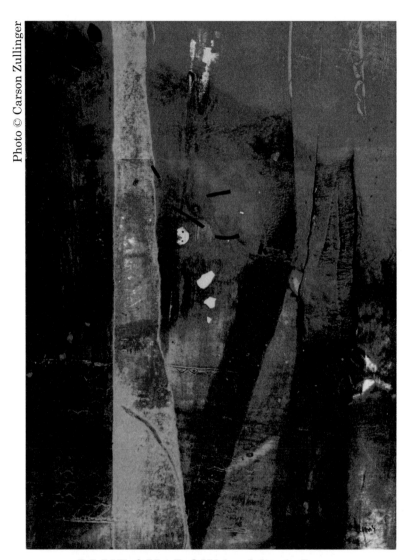

BLUE SHADOW by Mitch Lyons

Essays
Interviews
Photographs

The CREATIVE
Landscape of AGING

Judith Zausner

This book is dedicated to everyone everywhere who is a creative pioneer. Take risks, be courageous, think outside the box. Play a lot. Please accept my wishes for an artful life filled with love, kindness, and integrity.

Judith Zausner

"Creativity is contagious. Pass it on."

Albert Einstein

DISCLAIMER:
Every effort has been made to accurately portray people, events, and art. Please understand that the essays as well as the interviews have taken place over a period of years so in addition to the change of an artist's age, there may be changes in circumstance. Furthermore, every effort has been used to correctly identify and credit the art by the artist as well as the photographer of the art. This book has involved substantial research time and many one-on-one conversations. If there is a possible omission or an error, please excuse that as it is not intentional.

Cover Design: Nuno Moreira, NMDESIGN.ORG
Interior Design: Leslie Bauman Design
Editor: Peter Schwarz

Contents

Essays: Guiding Creativity

Interviews

Gallery

Endnotes

Forward

The Creative Landscape of Aging is a compelling title not only for those interested in creativity, but also for those who are actively considering how they want to live the third stage of their lives. In reading Judith Zausner's book, it is intriguing to consider the words in the title as verbs—create, landscape, and age. If you are a "boomer" or approaching the third stage of your life, you may want to ask: What do I want to create for this stage of my life? What do I want to accomplish? What part does creativity play in my life? I know you will find the articles Zausner has written and the artists she has interviewed to be helpful guides in answering these questions.

The "landscape" or terrain of aging is not static and keeps changing. My mother, an avid gardener who sold rare books on horticulture, knew that landscapes present certain "givens." However, within those "givens," there were many choices she could make. She knew how to work with the land to create a landscape she would find pleasing—what to plant, how to design it, how to build on its best features, and how to tend to it. She created beautiful gardens, and her artistry shone—particularly in gardening and landscaping. Me, not so much, but I think the analogy is an apt one.

We all are the artists of our lives and create the landscapes we live in. My mother continued to live a vibrant and interesting life as she grew older. She knew the importance of dealing with the inevitable changes that occur during our lives and as we age. At her memorial service, my sister wrote a letter she had written explaining change as one of life's "givens"—"everything changes, even the rocks we find in the garden." People fortunate enough to engage in creative activities have the ability to evolve and grow through life's changes.

While there are certain "givens," we all have the freedom to choose how we will live our lives. Obstacles arise, we go on "detours," events happen that we did not plan. While we experience disruptions during all phases of our lives, aging presents unique challenges. We may encounter health challenges we haven't had before. We realize time is limited. What is the best way to accomplish what we still have to do? What part does creativity play in the third stage of our lives?

To meet dissertation requirements for a graduate degree that focused on creativity, I interviewed people ranging in age from 66 to 102 years old who were engaged in creative activities spanning a number of disciplines including writing, visual arts, and music. While participants had achieved success in their creative activities, none were considered "famous." I was interested to know if creative activities helped participants complete developmental tasks of their later years, provided meaning, and helped them cope with challenges of aging.

When I reviewed theories of adult development, I found certain themes in common: 1) adult development is ongoing; 2) development is a change, growth, or learning process; 3) there is a continual process of incorporating what fits from present or previous phases of knowing and a letting go of ideas that no longer apply; and 4) the last period of adult development requires a summing up of life so that one can move on to a period which includes generativity and transcendence. In short, developmental tasks of the later years include spiritual issues such as developing wisdom, unity and wholeness, facing death and transcendence.

What I learned from in-depth interviews, questionnaires, and instruments administered to the creators I studied is they had a framework for their lives, were fulfilling their goals, believed their lives had meaning, and shared many of the characteristics of self-actualized people. On measures of meaning, life-fulfillment, and self-actualization, creative participants scored significantly higher than the normative data for the general population. Through interviews I conducted, I learned that involvement in creative activities was a crucial part of their lives and that creativity was a conduit for achieving a life rich with meaning—despite some of the health challenges they faced as they grew older. Creative activities helped them continue to grow, develop, change, and take risks. They were "authentic individuals" because they defined themselves, had a strong sense of presence, and knew who they were. When they encountered setbacks, their creative activities motivated them to "go with the flow" and keep on going. The creative adults I interviewed described creativity as a "gift" and a "blessing."

I am certain the creators Zausner interviews experience the beneficial aspects of creativity as well—in addition to being caught up in the sheer joy or "flow" they experience as they create. The exciting fact about creativity is that it is available to us all. While some of us may protest that we are not "creative" when we compare ourselves to famous creators, in recent years ideas of creativity have been expanded to include "everyday creativity." There have been numerous studies involving creativity, and the subject has been explored by many articles in the popular press. We have started to think of creativity as a great asset, not only because creative results add beauty and enjoyment to life, but creativity is seen as part of our evolution as a species and a skill necessary for survival.

I had a recent and poignant reminder of the role creativity can play in our very survival when my husband and I wandered through Aslilah, an artistic little fishing village close to Tangier in Morocco. The village, which had been conquered by the Portuguese in 1471, retained a Portuguese feel with whitewashed buildings and ornamental doors and doorways. As we turned a corner of a winding street, we saw a woman who had painted the bright doors of her town on little pieces of plywood that were spread out on the blanket she sat on. As we stopped to admire her charming works of art, I realized the woman's arms ended in stumps and she had no hands. In spite of her obvious physical challenges, she had managed to create her paintings by holding a brush with her teeth and used her toes as fingers. When I bought one of her paintings, she realized she had not signed it. With a pen in her toes, she signed her name, Karima, on the back of her painting!

While Karima may offer an extraordinary example of the role creativity can play in our very survival, we all can give examples of how creativity can sustain us, give us hope, and contribute meaning despite difficulties we may face as we age. I have watched as my husband, John, who has Parkinson's disease, finds beauty and joy in life through his photographs, art, and poetry writing despite challenges that accompany the disease. Michael, a friend with PD, writes, composes songs, and plays them on his guitar. The creative older adults I interviewed found joy and meaning through their creative activities, despite significant health challenges that included blindness, neurologic disorders, and lung disease.

Zausner, through her business Caring Crafts and experience conducting craft workshops, is an expert on making creative activities accessible to older adults and those with special needs. I had the privilege of assisting her at one of the workshops she conducted for older adults and was impressed with her wealth of knowledge of famous artists who created despite their challenges and the "hands-on" involvement in creative activities through craft options she presented. Her book is an opportunity to experience what she has learned through her business, the workshops she has conducted, her writings and interviews with mature artists.

The people I interviewed believed that creativity

was an imperative—to develop themselves, to develop their spirits, and to make the world a better place. Byproducts of their creative activities were involvement in life, the joy of discovery, and lives lived with enthusiasm and passion. They formed supportive relationships and did all they could to create a favorable landscape to support their creativity. They knew time was short, and they acted wisely. As one artist said, "I don't go down false roads anymore."

—*Christina Robertson, PhD*
Creativity and Aging:

A Grounded Theory Study of Creative Older Adults

Introduction

Think left and think right and think low and think high. Oh, the thinks you can think up if only you try!

Dr. Seuss

It took almost sixty years. No, I was not patient at all.

After college, I chose a graduate program in Occupational Therapy. It was logical; I enjoyed the sciences, helping people, and doing creative work. When I realized the creative element was not fostered, I took a quick leap out and then searched for that right mix for my career. Not easy. I went in and out of corporate positions as well as entrepreneurial ventures looking for a lasting fit. While each opportunity provided a learning experience, I also learned that my frustration had no bounds. I was always optimistic and always disappointed.

Then one summer evening at the age of 59, I had an epiphany. I had met a woman my age who, only a couple of years earlier, had unfortunately been stricken with Multiple Sclerosis. It was aggressive for her, and she walked with arm braces. I inquired about her home therapy visits, and she said that she placed pegs in holes. Interested, I wondered what else she had been guided with, and the answer came back, "Nothing else." I was shocked and in disbelief. So that evening I went online, determined to find creative alternatives for her therapy but found nothing. And that is when the epiphany happened. There must be thousands and thousands of compromised individuals relegated to simple rote exercises that do not engage the mind, spirit, or soul, and definitely not creative imagination. And so I was determined to change that landscape and offer proprietary craft kits that were creatively based, easy to make, required no precision, and produced terrific results.

I registered my Caring Crafts business and established a website *(www.caringcrafts.com)* that would sell both kits and safe tools.

Initially I focused on adults of all ages with all levels and types of cognitive and/or physical impairments. Then through my marketing efforts, I met professionals who were working in various capacities with older adults. It was clearly a fast growing demographic with special and diverse needs. I began to read about what was happening in this field and became very excited by the range of studies that involved the creative process. The late Dr. Gene Cohen (George Washington University) was at the forefront of validating the benefits of creativity for older adults. In one study, he established two separate groups of adults aged 65 and older; one carried on with their normal routines, and the other adults were infused with creative experiences. Dr. Cohen found that those who were in the creative group were less depressed, needed fewer doctor visits and medications, fell less frequently, and in general experienced better health and were more active socially. Dr. Cohen concluded, "Community-based cultural programs for older adults appear to be reducing risk factors that drive the need for long-term care."

Above Ground was another study that was of special interest and was led by Joan Jeffri at Columbia University. She studied older artists living in New York City to evaluate their approach to aging. Jeffri found that they do not retire, but live active full lives by going to their studios and working daily. If a walk used to be short, and now it takes significantly longer, it does not deter the artist from getting to his/her place of work. These artists are determined, savvy, and have an intense creative drive.

These two studies were exciting news for me. In fact, Dr. Cohen played an integral part in the founding of the National Center for Creative Aging in Washington, DC.

With this information on aging and creativity and my new business launch, I began exploring the field. I knew that the aging population was growing exponentially and that the creative wheel was critical in maintaining physical health and morale. I began meeting and corresponding with many people in the field and began to write, then offer talks and workshops. I knew that my Caring Crafts mission to empower creativity and abilities had found a focus.

After my first article appeared on a website, I wrote more and started my blog: *Creativity Matters (www.agingandcreativity.blogspot.com)*. It is entirely based on unique aspects of creativity with pervasive content on the older adult. Then I met a remarkable elderly artist, Marie Ulmer, who was in her 90s and became a frequent workshop participant. I was fascinated by her agility, focus, and skill, and I decided to interview her for my blog. That was my first interview. I learned so much about Marie in the process and slowly started to seek out other older visual artists for interviews.

Talking to people and hearing their artistic journeys was very compelling, and at some point I decided to publish this book, which combines these interviews with my essays on creative perspectives.

Many people have asked me what type of art I make, and my answer is that I am a "creative generalist." I explore many mediums and prefer to respond creatively and spontaneously to opportunities without being defined as painter or sculptor or illustrator or weaver. Currently I am enjoying hat making and selling them in art centers in Philadelphia.

This journey of immersion with the creative and aging sector has been wonderful. Over the past six years, I have met so many involved, smart, and caring people who have welcomed me in the field with interest and respect. I hope that my work resonates with many people who read this book and feel inspired by the stories. I also hope that in this field I have left a positive footprint.

So there are many people and organizations to thank.

National Mature Media Awards for numerous recognitions of my writing for the mature audience.

Suzanne Roberts, host of Seeking Solutions with Suzanne on Comcast TV, for inviting me on her show to demonstrate my Caring Crafts kits.

Philadelphia Corporation of Aging for the opportunity to provide presentations and workshops at annual events.

Dick Goldberg at Coming of Age for the opportunity of writing for Coming of Age and announcing my events in their newsletter.

Megan Joyce, the editor of *50plus Senior News*, for providing a column for me to publish many of my articles.

National Center for Creative Aging for the opportunity to actively contribute to the launch of their blog.

Global Alliance for Arts & Health (formerly The Society for the Arts in Healthcare) for providing a consultancy grant for Caring Crafts right after I opened the cyber doors.

American Society on Aging for their interest and publication of my writing.

Dick Levinson at the Free Library in Philadelphia for contracting my talks for his senior audience.

Ralston Center for their generous support of my creativity workshops using crafts for older adults.

David Bunnell, who was the first person to ask me to write about my work for the eldr.com website, which unfortunately has since closed its cyber doors.

Chris Robertson, friend and colleague in the aging and creativity sector, for her interest in my work and generosity of including me in her professional world. I am very touched by her Forward for this book.

Laura Marmar, a friend, who is keenly aware of my interest and keeps me informed of relevant information in the art world.

Tobi Zausner, my sister whose interview is in this book, has been a great source of information and my personal cheerleader. Her book, *When Walls Be-*

come Doorways, is about talented artists of all ages who have had a serious health crisis and have found their way back successfully to their creative passion. She is a recognized expert in psychology and a very talented artist.

The physical book could not have happened without the extraordinary help and dedication to the project by my editor, Peter Schwarz, and my art director, Leslie Bauman. There are so many details in bringing this work to book form, and they have used their talent and support to make this book happen.

I would like to thank all the artists whom I had the privilege to interview. They have taken the time to share their compelling stories and their interest in my project to inspire others. Please note that their ages as well as other time-sensitive information was accurate at the time the interviews were written, but has not been altered to reflect the date of this book's publication. In addition, all information on the essays is reflective of the date on which it was first published.

Finally my children, Anneliese and Tavish, who hold a very special place in my heart, have been witness to my roller coaster professional journey and have always been steadfast with their love, respect, and kindness.

—*Judith Zausner*

ESSAYS
Living a Creative Life

Imagination, Creativity, and Confidence

*We all live every day in virtual environments,
defined by our ideas.*

Michael Crichton

I dream of painting and then I paint my dream.

Vincent van Gogh

It is the perfect triad: imagination, creativity, and confidence. Imagination is the cognitive state of dreaming up new ideas or solutions; creativity is the process of developing those innovative thoughts into action; and confidence happens as a result of making those dreams a reality. It's a simple equation that constitutes a complex series of events. It may take minutes, days, or even years to produce the final project, but completion provides closure and builds confidence. Self-efficacy is an important concept here because it embraces the belief that your actions can make a difference in producing expected results.

We all have dreams and fantasies, hopes and aspirations, and that makes us different from other living creatures. So what sets us apart from each other is that some people can raise their emotional capital and intellectual stamina to seize an opportunity to become innovative. Driven by a thirst for new challenges, they unconsciously disregard feelings of fear and inadequacy. These are people who embrace the unknown and understand that thinking outside the box is about finding the unpredictable, problem-solving, and being on the winning side of the creative experience.

In her book, *When Walls Become Doorways,* Dr. Tobi Zausner writes about how difficult life events can transform an individual and their creative process. As a young woman, Frida Kahlo suffered massive bodily injuries from a bus accident and was restricted to bed for many months. Her mother had a special easel built that could be used by someone lying down, and her father gave her oil paint. "Lying in bed, Kahlo started to create the paintings that would eventually make her famous," says Zausner. Kahlo channeled her passion and talent and became a celebrated artist.

Thanks to a dream Elias Howe had, he realized how to fasten the needle and cloth together on the sewing machine he was developing. "I was taken prisoner by a group of natives. They were dancing around with spears. As they were moving around me, I noticed their spears all had holes near their tips." Although the dream was frightening, he translated the dream to make his invention work. By placing a hole near the tip of the needle so thread could pass through, fabric could be sewn on the machine. This is a classic example of how imagination can initiate the creative process and result in confidence as a result of its success.

Sometimes being in a compelling profession inspires thoughts for another creative outlet. Both Michael Crichton (*Jurassic Park, ER* television series) and John Grisham (*A Time to Kill, Pelican Brief*) had careers in medicine and law, respectively. In their work, both surely had "what if" moments that developed into a string of possibilities as a mental narrative. That started their writing careers, which spawned such popular novels that they left their professions and devoted themselves to writing. Grisham says, "I seriously doubt I would ever have written the first story had I not been a lawyer. I never dreamed of being a writer. I wrote only after witnessing a trial."

Sometimes a dream can be so prescient that it requires verification in reality. "I woke up with a lovely tune in my head," Paul McCartney recalled to his biographer, Barry Miles. "I thought, 'That's great. I wonder what that is?'" He got up that morning in May, 1965, went to the piano, and began playing the melody that would become "Yesterday." While he really liked the tune, he had some reservations: "Because I'd dreamed it, I couldn't believe I'd written it." [1] It took two weeks to add lyrics, and it became one of the most popular songs in history, having been voted the #1 pop song of all time by MTV and *Rolling Stone Magazine*. The song was also inducted into the Grammy Hall of Fame.

Age and talent are not as important as drive in bringing your imagination to an active state of creativity. You can build up your confidence with each process and with every success, no matter how small. So dream, aspire, play, and allow yourself to make plenty of mistakes. Be flexible, go with the flow, get lost experimenting. Find the fun, enjoy yourself, and trust the process.

"Imagination, Creativity, and Confidence" originally appeared on July 18, 2010 at *http://agingand-creativity.blogspot.com/2010/07/imagination-creativity-confidence.html*.

Creative Thinking and Positive Aging

Our greatest glory is not in never falling,
but in rising every time we fall.

Confucius

We all have them, and we all hate them. Problems. It takes our time, saps our energy, and puts us in a negative space. But only temporarily. We usually find a solution and move on. And yet there are times when that problem is actually an unrealized gift.

Alexander Graham Bell said, "When one door closes, another opens; but we often look so long and so regretfully upon the closed door that we do not see the one which has opened for us." Enter mental flexibility, creative thinking, and positive psychology, a triad of intellectual ammunition that can transform battles to opportunities. Well-known successes have been launched with this approach, and our lives are better because of it. Many famous people, despite their initial failures, did not give up; instead they regrouped, rethought, recharged, and came back with new strategies. For example, Henry Ford failed and went broke five times before he had success. R. H. Macy failed seven times before his New York City store became a valued retailer. Walt Disney went bankrupt several times before he built Disneyland.

These people worked on long term goals; they fell and got up again many times before they reached the finishing line. They were creative thinkers, tenacious with their vision, yet flexible in their thought processes. Eventually their success reaped not only financial benefits, but also personal satisfaction. Their triumph became our benefit.

As we age, our hurdles are more focused on our physical changes and less on career challenges. Everyone has a different way of coping—meditation, prayer, support groups, and denial are avenues that will often alleviate some stress. There are many instances of older adults who realized that if they maintained their focus and looked at their problem from a different angle, a new solution, perhaps even a serendipitous one, could provide a new source of joy to their lives. Here are some examples:

• Don R. is a retired Professor of Literature. He

has read and re-read classics many times as well as thousands of other books because reading has been an integral part of his life. But when his eyesight began to fail him, real frustration was on the horizon. Enter audio books. Don has become so engaged in this new way of consuming literature that he feels it offers benefits that reading quietly by himself does not. For instance, when he listens to poetry, he can actually hear the cadence rather than silently read it. So Don, analytical by nature, evaluates narrators as critically as many evaluate authors, and he enjoys talking about their differences, addressing valuable insights to the theatre of the written word.

- Jane S. loves Florida and her senior community. She has always been independent and enjoys driving to see friends and doing errands. However, when her quick response time slowed down, her stress on the road escalated, and her fender benders added to her insurance expense. Jane knew that she had to stop driving, but she did not want to stop being on the go. At the same time, her physician was concerned about her weight gain and sedentary lifestyle. The solution was evident: bike riding. Although she had not ridden in years, she took it up quickly again and can be seen pedaling around her community to see friends while losing weight, feeling better, and enjoying more confidence in herself.

- Jean E. founded a free dance program for youth. She choreographed and also designed and constructed the costumes. But when arthritis took hold, she needed to change her focus. "It had been a long life dream of hers to write a historical novel," her daughter said. To date, Jean has written four novels, and although she is now struggling with macular degeneration, true to her spirit, she is using the "best aids available at this time as she still has a couple more books brewing in her mind," reflected her daughter. Her upbeat attitude is an inspiration and shows that age and its physical changes cannot take away our creativity and desires to explore what life has to offer.

So it's possible, and definitely advantageous, to take those problems and create new positive experiences. "While simple cognitive processing measures such as those of memory and attention might decline with age, it seems that everyday problem solving does not."[2] We possess the experience and wisdom to make choices to better our life experience. While disappointments and hurdles will crop up, our decision to mine positive alternatives will support a healthier way of living. Everyday creativity is less about art and more about how we configure these choices and relate to the world around us. Creative thinking and perseverance will reap the rewards of positive aging.

"Creative Thinking and Positive Aging" original-ly appeared on July 31, 2011 at *http://agingand-creativity.blogspot.com/2011/07/creative-think-ing-positive-aging.html*. This article received a Na-tional Mature Media Award.

When Creative Success Comes Later in Life

I have learned that if one advances confidently in the direction of his dreams, and endeavors to live the life he has imagined, he will meet with a success unexpected in common hours.

Henry David Thoreau

Some have struggled for years in jobs, others have followed a quiet creative life, and there are many individuals who have tenaciously held on to their entrepreneurial spirit. Yet creative success found them later in life. When you have dreams of something beyond your present experience, patience is your biggest friend.

Here are some examples:

- Anna Mary Robertson ("Grandma" Moses) was in her 70s when she began painting scenes of her rural life in upstate New York. This self-taught artist, mother, and widow became one of the most famous American folk artists of the 20th Century and continued painting in her 90s.

- Louise Nevelson was in her 50s when she sold her work to three New York City museums, and now her art can be seen internationally in over eighty public collections. Shortly before her 60th birthday, she became President of the Artist's Equity New York chapter, which was the first of many art leadership positions she would attain.

- When she was just months shy of her 50th birthday, Julia Child collaborated on her first French cooking book, a two-volume set titled *Mastering the Art of French Cooking*. Soon after, she promoted her book on television and that catapulted her overnight sensation in the culinary world.

- Colonel Sanders of finger lickin' good chicken fame had a difficult start in life but early on realized he had a creative cooking talent. However it was not until he was in his 60s that he started KFC and became a millionaire.

- Up until the age of 40, devoutly religious Anton Bruckner composed music solely for the Catholic Church. Then a meeting with Wagner turned his life around, and he began to compose symphonies of epic proportion. He was working on his great Symphony No. 9 when he died at 72.

- Elliot Carter has received media attention at age 100. A review from *The New York Times* music critic was in praise of his latest, centenarian work, *Interventions*, describing it as "lucidly textured, wonderfully inventive, even impish. This was the work of a living master in full command."

- Laura Ingalls Wilder wrote about her family's life in the 1870s and 1880s in the acclaimed *The Little House on the Prairie* series of books for children. She published her first book at the age of 65.

- Harry Bernstein was in his 90s when he decided to write his memoirs after his wife of sixty-seven years died. He titled his book *The Invisible Wall: A Love Story That Broke Barriers* and continued to write with the recently published book *The Dream*.

- Louis Kahn, a Russian immigrant, was an important architect of the 20th Century. He created his first important piece of architecture, the Yale University Art Gallery, when he was in his 50s. He continued to design notable academic buildings.

- As a jobless architect during the Depression, Alfred Mosher Butts invented Scrabble which became the most popular word game in the world. He did not realize success of the game until his early 50s when the Chairman of the Macy's department store placed a large order and promoted it.

- Charles Darwin was 50 years old when he published his complete theory of evolution in *On the Origin of Species*, which sold out the first day it was released and subsequently had six editions. He continued to write for at least ten more years (e.g., *The Descent of Man*).

- André Kertész was born in Hungary, and after years in France photographing artists, he immigrated to the US. Now remembered as an eminent photojournalist, his career vacillated until, at the age of 70, he had a solo show at the Museum of Modern Art and subsequently in galleries all over the world.

This is a short list of many people in a variety of creative venues who pursued their passion and realized success at age 50 and beyond. Their achievements took many paths, twists and turns, and surely there were moments of self-doubt. Coming from a broad range of socioeconomic backgrounds—Charles Darwin never had to earn a living while Laura Ingalls Wilder grew up with few resources—their privileged status was not a common thread. But these late bloomers all share an exceptional ability to persevere, a brilliant talent that would not lay quiet, a set of good genes, and a stable environment. They have enriched our lives as a result of their determination and unwavering spirit, and they challenge those who believe that old age is simply a negative consequence of living.

"When Creative Success Comes Later in Life" originally appeared on March 29, 2009 at *http://agingandcreativity.blogspot.com/2009/03/when-creative-success-comes-later-in.html*. This article won a National Mature Media Award.

Celebrating Your Legacy

*In the power to change yourself is the power
to change the world around you.*

Anwar al-Sadat

"Legacy is as public as an architectural monument and as private as a letter written to children or grandchildren. It's as tangible as a bank check and as intangible as a seemingly casual word of advice. And it's as life enhancing as the Heimlich maneuver and as life denying as the Holocaust," says Meg Newhouse, PhD.

My interest is in our personal legacy; in the passion, purpose and commitment that creates an indelible mark on the human landscape when we are no longer here to be part of it. It takes courage and kindness, dedication and fortitude to make that reach that will make a difference. Most people are not born famous and then leave a legacy; they become famous after they achieved success in their world of change. Clara Barton (formed the American Red Cross), Mother Teresa (advocate for the poor and helpless), Jonas Salk (developed Polio vaccine), and Christiaan Barnard (engineered the first heart transplant) all believed that healing others was their mission. They were dedicated to their work and as a result have helped people all over the world in perpetuity.

Here are some current examples of legacies:

Social entrepreneur and author Marc Freedman established Civic Ventures to support social change by recognizing the experience of older adults and encouraging personal and professional renewal.[3] Under civic ventures, multiple programs are offered, including The Purpose Prize which awards individuals age 60 and over for social innovation and their approach to solving some of the world's biggest problems. The "experience dividend" has propelled many to create "greater good in the second half of life." [4]

Dr. Gene Cohen, MD, PhD passed away in 2009, but his legacy in the world of creativity and aging is enormous.[5] He was the leading professional to offer research studies and writings that fully supported the premise of positive aging as a result of a creative lifestyle. (Books include *The Mature Mind: The Positive Power of the Aging Brain* and *The Creative*

Age: Awakening Human Potential in the Second Half of Life.) His groundbreaking studies have built a nationwide movement that owes its presence and strength to his work.

Alexandra Scott (b.1992) was one year old when she was diagnosed with cancer.[6] Unable to conquer the disease, Alex wanted a lemonade stand so she could make money to help fund a cure. Although she passed away at the age of eight, her legacy has encouraged products and events that have raised many millions of dollars for research. Her three brothers continue her work through their commitment to her legacy with Alex's Lemonade Stand Foundation.

J.A. and Geraldine Reynolds lost their son, Bruce, who was a patrolman for the Port Authority of New York on 9/11.[7] He was an extraordinary and charismatic person who loved to garden. Shortly after 9/11, the New York City Department of Parks & Recreation delivered daffodils to plant in Reynolds' community garden in New York City's Isham Park. Now The Daffodil Project "is the largest volunteer, citizen-driven planting effort in New York City's history, with over 20,000 participants planting 2.5 million flowers since the Fall of 2001."

Nancy Lublin started Dress for Success in 1996 with three nuns from Spanish Harlem and a $5,000 inheritance from her great-grandfather.[8] Today this worldwide non-profit organization promotes "the economic independence of disadvantaged women by providing professional attire, a network of support and the career development tools to help women thrive in work and in life." Through generous donations of clothes and accessories, financial contributions, and paid staff and volunteers, Dress for Success has helped over 500,000 women.

Our lives are a blizzard of experiences and many responses are automatic. The phone rings, and we pick it up, we drive the same route daily and never look at street names, and we're moving from point A to point B and wondering where C is while preparing to get to point G. What makes us unique, however, and what makes living special is our intention to give meaning to our lives. People have all sorts of gifts and responses to the world around them. Some will leave creative products in art, music, and writing as their legacy, but most people will leave intangible legacies that are founded on direct social engagement. It can be volunteering at a soup kitchen or hospital, or working on fundraising campaigns for a favorite charity, or rescuing stray dogs or cats to find them shelter. It can be helping neighbors or friends who are less fortunate, or helping in a community center or school. Involvement can alter lives and begin a legacy. Fred Mandell, PhD, writer, artist, and personal catalyst, says, "Doubt, frustration, and fear are part of life's journey, but they are not as powerful as passion, commitment and purpose."

For a legacy to be strong, your passion, purpose, and commitment must be strong; waiting for tomorrow is not as effective as doing it today. The time is now to build your legacy so it will represent your life and your spirit of caring.

Celebrate yourself. Celebrate your legacy.

"Celebrating Your Legacy" originally appeared on December 19, 2009 at *http://agingandcreativity.blogspot.com/2009/12/celebrating-your-legacy.html.*

Hope, Creativity, and Change

If you lose hope, somehow you lose the vitality that keeps life moving, you lose that courage to be, that quality that helps you go on in spite of it all. And so today I still have a dream.

Martin Luther King, Jr.

Hope is the positive force that propels us forward. With hope, there is an expectation of something we want to happen. We use it everyday: waiting impatiently for a bus to come and hoping it appears in the next minute, caring for a sick friend and hoping that s/he will get better soon, enjoying an indulgence in sweets and hoping to regain will power tomorrow to resume dieting, etc. Mentally we allow ourselves to flex to the possibilities of change. We imagine and create scenarios to fill our needs and desires. Having the mental freedom to conceive and dream of these changes is an integral part of our creative thought processes. We give ourselves permission to dream a little so that we can subconsciously will an event, a person, an experience to change and make a wonderful difference in our lives. Without hope, we're relegated to the doldrums of life and open to helplessness, despair, and depression.

With hope comes change and with change comes innovation. It is a simple flow chart. America captured this symbolically with the election of Barack Obama as our next President. We voted for "change we can believe in" because we needed a new rudder to guide us safely through the current economic turbulence and other domestic problems. In support of Obama, the well-known Pop artist Robert Indiana (at age 79) designed the sculpture *Hope* as a graphic similar to his famous *LOVE* artwork (with the letter "O" on a diagonal).[9] But what if Barack did not have hope? What if two years ago, with little money or endorsements and minimal support by the polls and pundits, Barack despaired and no longer believed that he could gain enough support of voters to become President? Fortunately, his campaign mantra, the power of three affirmative words, "Yes, we can!" resonated strongly across the nation and across political divides to bring victory.[10] It was based on hope and not fear, on change and not the status quo.

Hope is also a survival tool. In 2002, Laurie Johnson survived a plane crash but lost her husband and young son in the accident. Left with a severely broken leg, Laurie faced a long process of rehabilitation, which included multiple surgeries and prolonged use of crutches. With physical and emotional struggles, she hoped that she could get back to her life prior to the accident. Bored with the dismal, dull grayness of crutches, she and her sister started to play creatively with change. Their ideas ignited a new business that embraced crutches with fashion and comfort, and LemonAid Crutches was born.[11] Crutches and arm pads are now available in fun and elegant styles and provide valued comfort as well as visual pleasure.

Hope means replacing the old and choosing something new. It's an opportunity for the heart and mind to flex together creatively and be an explorer in an unknown land. It's a voluntary challenge we pursue when convention no longer makes sense and the new road is like a beautiful untouched path of fresh snow.

"Hope, Creativity, and Change" originally appeared on November 17, 2008 at *http://agingand-creativity.blogspot.com/2008/11/hope-creativity-change.html.*

Am I an Artist?

Academic degrees are not required. There are no certifications. But it is anticipated that you bring passion, dedication, and talent to the profession. Do you have it?

Art can be tangible or intangible, practical or impractical, private or public, appreciated or disregarded. Making art exists in a vast arena with no license. But that does not make it easy; it has to satisfy. To be an artist, you have to create and love to create and feel compelled to create. However, the process of considering yourself an artist is an inward journey.

Li Gardiner struggled with the concept of taking on the role of an artist and says, "Today, if you ask me who I am, or what I do, I will tell you easily and naturally, 'I am an artist.' It wasn't always easy. It took years of doubt to get to this point, but I figured out how to maintain my belief in myself as an artist, in the face of all obstacles." [12]

How can you consider yourself an artist? Many people have pictures in their mind of what an artist looks like, how they dress, the way they live, and of course what they create. It roots from our knowledge of master painters such as Michelangelo, Renoir, Picasso, artists who captured subjects on canvas with their expertise and vision. Comparing yourself to a famous artist may not be an exercise in elevating your self-esteem, but by studying and emulating their techniques, you can improve your work. We're all different; our abilities, sensitivities, and styles make us unique. By developing your talent, believing in your art and securing your confidence, you will be prepared to succeed. Buddha claims, "We are what we think. All that we are arises with our thoughts. With our thoughts, we make our world."

If you take that inner journey to be an artist, you must fill the path with focus. The dedication and drive required cannot be overestimated. Joan Jeffri's project, *Above Ground: Information on Artists III: Special Focus New York City Aging Artists*, studied a group of artists from 62 to 97 years old. [13] Jeffri sums up her findings: "All the artists we interviewed visited their studios on a frequent and sometimes daily basis, even if it took 1.5 hours to walk the three blocks to the studio. When the medium became too taxing—such as large-scale sculpture or paintings, not one artist talked of giving up art; s/he simply changed the medium." This is not uncommon for prolific and committed artists to continue to pursue making art no matter what hurdles lie in their path. In her book, *When Walls Become Doorways*, Tobi Zausner describes the creative spirit of artists who overcame physical obstacles to continue their work.[14] An example is Matisse, who, confined to his bed or wheelchair, drew on walls and, with charcoal attached to a fishing pole, also drew on the ceiling.

With talent, you create. With passion, you commit. Are you an artist?

"Am I an Artist?" originally appeared on September 23, 2010 at *http://agingandcreativity.blogspot.com/2010/09/am-i-artist.html*.

This article was originally written at the request of *www.artsyshark.com*.

Happiness, Creativity, and the Older Adult

Happiness is big business. Hundreds of thousands of books in print, billions of dollars spent in pills and psychotherapy visits, and yet it remains temporary and for some elusive. Mental health is based on responding appropriately to experiences and, with life's ups and downs, no sane person can be happy one hundred percent of the time. So we fluctuate. We are happy, and then we are unhappy and then find happiness again. We desire euphoria even though it does not have the stability of an inanimate object or the permanence of a tattoo.

Happiness research provides surprising data. Harvard psychologist Dan Gilbert says a year after a person wins the lottery and a year after a person becomes paraplegic and loses functions of his/her legs, their happiness quota is the same.[15] Remarkable. He says research has shown that most traumatic events longer than three months past will lose their impact and duration with a person. Gilbert theorizes that it is our being able to synthesize happiness and that we adjust to create happiness. For example, in his article, "Aging Artists on the Creativity of Their Old Age," Dr. Martin Lindauer quotes a female artist in her 60s: "I can no longer make very large projects, but making things can be rewarding also. My energy has diminished somewhat, and a lot of time has been lost recovering from surgery, but I have never stopped working. I have a compulsion to make things of my own design. I am fortunate in that my mind seems to be intact." This woman uses her positive attitude consistently by recognizing the problem, creating positive acceptance (synthesizing happiness), and moving forward with gratitude. It also exemplifies her flexible and resilient approach to living.

So we have opportunity to be happy through a genuine experience (e.g., winning the lottery) or a synthetically adjusted experience. However happiness comes to you, numerous studies have shown that those who profess to be happy tend to be optimistic, unencumbered by failure or the unknown, more social and experience greater control of their lives. When you are feeling good, life is easier and more fun; the sun is always shining. It's easier to tackle projects and anticipate success because failure and fear are not on your dashboard. To explore and discover, to socialize with others, and to be the positive rudder in your life, is empowering and enabling. We view life through a different lens.

Psychologist Adam Anderson's studies have shown the value of being happy in our approach to processing information around us. "With positive mood, you actually get more access to things you would normally ignore," he says. "Instead of looking through a porthole, you have a landscape or panoramic view of the world."[16]

This is excellent fodder for creativity, which requires unique thinking to incorporate sometimes disparate elements, for an optimal solution. When you are feeling upbeat you can embrace your world, respond positively to elements and are therefore more open and flexible to integrating them. The creative experience provides challenge as well as satisfaction and often a sense of exhilaration. You are the owner, the maker, the problem-solver.

Susanne Matthiesen, M.B.A, writes about Virginia Hall, an older artist who responds to Eleanor Roosevelt's advice ("Do something every day that scares you"): A professional artist since her retirement, Hall continues to find exhilaration in the 'scary' places of art. "I don't know of a better way to achieve a scary moment than to engage the creative process," she says.[17]

Hall compares life to her artwork metaphysically. "It's somewhat of an illusion to think that you're making something. Oh, yes, you can paint a canvas or form a piece of clay. Ultimately, you're seeking a discovery," she says. "The point isn't the experience itself, but how it affects your sense of well-being and self-expression. Look within and around yourself."

Creativity is an integral part of aging well; it facilitates wellness through enhanced self-esteem and socialization. Amy Gorman, author of *Aging Artfully,* has profiled artists from 85 years old to 107 years old and says, "The women artists demonstrate for Boomers and the rest of us, that there are ways to promote healthy aging through a positive attitude."[18]

A positive attitude and a happy disposition are important in responding to the inherent hurdles of healthy aging. It is an active tool to combat everyday stress that can lead to depression and illness. Instead of seeing problems, contented people often perceive them as challenges to approach and overcome. Creativity is a tool that can fuel happiness and ward off depression. A study co-sponsored by George Washington University and the National Endowment for the Arts found that adults aged 65 and over who were continuously participating in arts programs were documented to have fewer doctors' visits, require less medication, and were less apt to be depressed.

We cannot simply turn on and off the happiness switch inside ourselves, but we can strive to find happiness in our lives as much as possible. It feels great, promotes our creative thinking, and benefits our health.

The old adage "Don't worry, be happy" is a great mantra for us all.

"Happiness, Creativity, and the Older Adult" was originally published in the November-December 2010 issue of *Aging Today*, the bimonthly newspaper of the American Society on Aging, San Francisco, California. This essay appeared online on January 13, 2011 at *http://agingandcreativity.blogspot.com/2011/01/happiness-creativity-and-older-adult.html.*

Creativity, Conformity, and Aging

We don't stop playing because we grow old.
We grow old because we stop playing.

George Bernard Shaw

Creativity is about taking risks to make something new; to explore, conceive, develop, dream of something that has not existed before. There are no rules except those which may be inherent in a product that must function. On the contrary, conformity is all about rules and staying within boundaries. This can mean masking your persona to adapt in a job or social group so you are accepted by its commonalities. It can be especially true in organizational structures where politics play an important role and maintaining the group's expectations and invisible guidelines are paramount. Peer pressure to conform is with us from childhood on to our later years. However, psychologist Robert Ornstein (author of *The Psychology of Consciousness*), says, "If you spend too much time being like everybody else, you decrease your chances of coming up with something different." Although creativity and conformity are different entities, some people have been able to dream, conform, and succeed. It's about having a vision and knowing that it will fit in the world around you.

Inspired by seeing a voluptuous doll on the market in Germany, Ruth Handler made some observations. She saw that her daughter was playing with adult paper dolls rather than children and babies and that these dolls were all flat-chested. So in 1959, she designed her first Barbie doll, an attractive, small-scale plastic feminine figure with improbable proportions and breasts. Ruth thought young girls would enjoy role-playing with a three-dimensional doll fashioned to look stylish and youthful as they look toward their growing up years. She revolutionized the doll industry by creating a play figure that was completely different from any on the market, and she followed it by giving Barbie a boyfriend, Ken (both named for her children). It was a huge design leap, and yet her brilliant creativity was anchored in understanding the psychological needs of young girls. Ruth says, "The consumer made the Barbie doll an instant success."[19]

Thomas Edison held more patents than any other person in US history. Yet he was not your stereotypical reclusive and struggling inventor; he enjoyed collaboration and had six or more main assistants with unique expertise to help him. "One of Edison's greatest overlooked talents was his ability to assemble teams and set up an organizational structure that fostered many people's creativity," says historian Greg Field. He had a genius mind for creating new devices while relishing the group process where success of the group means conforming to the underlying group rules (perhaps his own). And his inventions needed to conform to society's needs in order to be successful.

Yet groups can thwart creativity. Jeremy Dean, a researcher at University College London, writes about Why Group Norms Kill Creativity.[20] "When groups are asked to think creatively the reason they frequently fail is because implicit norms constrain them in the most explicit ways. This is clearly demonstrated in a recent study carried out by Adarves-Yorno et al. (2006). They asked two groups of participants to create posters and subtly gave each group a norm about either using more words on the poster or more images.

"Afterwards when they judged each others' work,

participants equated creativity with following the group norm; the 'words' group rated posters with more words as more creative, and the 'images' group rated posters with more images as more creative. The unwritten rules of the group, therefore, determined what its members considered creative. In effect groups had redefined creativity as conformity."

So how does aging fit with creativity and conformity? There lies the paradox. As we age, we can continue to develop new neural networks if we are actively engaged in activities that may be social, creative, cognitive, and/or physical. Sure we can have memory lapses and concentration difficulties, but older adults also have beneficial neurological changes. Pattern recognition and more efficient brain signal transmission provides stronger problem-solving capability. And problem solving is integral to the creative process where there are many potential solutions and no fast conclusions. So it would appear that as mature adults we can be mentally wired for new explorations and more creativity, yet what halts so many? I believe it is fear of the unknown, unwilling to risk social exclusion, depression based on health concerns, and the comfort of their recliner. Motivation to seek new challenges is just as important as the discipline to eat nutritious food and exercise regularly. As Eric Maisel, PhD, creator of the *Meaning*

Solution Program, says, "Life feels more meaningful when you decide that your creativity matters."[21]

Conformity and creativity are part of the landscape of our lives. Finding ways to effectively manage them to strengthen our spirit as we age is a critical lesson for all of us.

"Creativity, Conformity, and Aging" originally appeared on March 14, 2010 at *http://agingandcreativity.blogspot.com/2010/03/creativity-conformity-and-aging.html.*

ESSAYS

Inspired Creativity

Innovative Technology Revolutionizes Prosthetic Legs

We must accept the proposition that humans are not disabled, a person can never be broken, our built environment and our technologies are broken. We, the people, need not accept these limitations, but can transcend disability through technological innovation.

Dr. Hugh Herr

Hugh Herr was a young expert level climber when, in 1982, he became disoriented during a blizzard on Mount Washington and suffered extreme frostbite, necessitating the amputation of both legs.[22]

Aimee Mullins was born without fibula bones, which required her legs to be amputated below the knee when she was 1 year old.[23]

Amy Purdy, an avid snowboarder, survived bacterial meningitis at the age of 19, but consequently lost hearing in one ear, kidney function, and both legs.[24]

Adrianne Haslet-Davis, a ballroom dancer and

instructor, was injured in the Boston Marathon bombing and lost part of her left leg.[25]

Mike "Monster Mike" Schultz lost his left leg above the knee in an accident during a snowmobile race.[26]

Gregg Stevenson lost both legs as a soldier in Afghanistan.[27]

All of these individuals have augmented their experience of being able-bodied. New technology has empowered them in ways that provide not only independent movement, but extreme movement and flexibility. They can jump higher than the average person and can run, dance, and move with natural grace.

Prior to his accident, Hugh Herr was not a focused student, but he took the accident to propel himself forward. Initially, it was to develop new feet for himself to better enable climbing, and then he advanced his technical work parallel with his academics. He says, "Nature is driving design and design is also driving nature. Bionics explores the interplay between biology and design; my legs are bionic and bionics has defined my physicality."

These are the three bionic interfaces integrated in design:

1. Mechanical: How things are attached to the body, e.g., for Hugh's legs they are attached using syn-

thetic skins and robotic tools.

2. Dynamic: Building bionic limbs to lift a person in to a stride. Exoskeletons being built will relieve the physical body demands, and therefore allow for extreme physical feats that will not impact metabolism

3. Electrical: Explores how it interfaces with the nervous system. Information is embedded in the chips of the bionic limb and is then under neural command.

Today Herr is Assistant Professor at MIT and head of the Biomechatronics research group at the MIT Media Lab, where he develops "wearable robotic systems that serve to augment human physical capability" and has Extreme Bionics as its center to advance the physical changes with the changes in the brain.[28] He no longer focuses on designs for himself, but for those who have difficulties that he can understand and possibly find a solution. Herr has published widely, holds many patents, and has received numerous awards for his remarkable work.

Aimee has had a lifetime of wearing prosthetic legs. Since a congenital defect left her without bones in her legs, she adjusted to what was available as she grew up. And she grew up to be a fashion model, actress, and athlete where she first received worldwide attention. An honor student, Aimee was one of three US students selected to receive a full academic scholarship from the Department of Defense and was the youngest person (at age 17) to have a top-secret security clearance at the Pentagon. As an athlete, she became the first amputee in national history to compete in the NCAA and also became the first person using woven carbon-fiber prostheses that were actually prototyped after the hind legs of a cheetah. The basic design of those cheetah legs became the global standard in sports prosthetics. Then the media discovered her, and she went on to become a fashion model as well as a spokesperson on beauty.

Aimee's engaging talk on TED explains the dynamics of her prosthetic legs as well as the choice of wearing any one of twelve different legs outfitted with different shoes or artful extensions on any day.[29]

Adrianne was with her husband, who had just returned from Afghanistan, walking around, and watching the Boston Marathon when the bomb went off only about four feet from where she was standing. She lost her foot and part of her leg. Recovery was grueling, but then she heard from *Dancing with the Stars,* which was exciting and gave her hope and focus to dance again. She performed at the 2014 TED Conference, which was her first time dancing in front of an audience since she was injured. Hugh Herr had designed her bionic leg specifically for dancing after he visited her in the hospital.[30]

Amy Purdy ignited *Dancing with the Stars* when she danced with Derek Hough in a steamy choreographed session.[31] Twirling and slithering around each other, Amy's permanently pointed rubber toed feet were initially designed for swimming, but magically brought grace in her dance movements. Her success is not limited to dance. As a competitive athlete, she won a bronze medal in snowboarding at the Sochi Paralympics. "If I can dance, I can walk. And if I can walk, I can snowboard. And I can live a great life," says Purdy.

Monster Mike, a professional athlete, is a Multi X Games Gold Medalist.[32] During a snowmobile race while pushing ahead of a competitor, his snowmobile turned over and severely damaged his left leg. As necessity is known to be the mother of invention, he created a prosthetic leg for himself. Without any engineering training, Mike used mountain bike parts to build his first prototype, and then enhanced the design so it would be adaptive to extreme sports. Using it while racing in adaptive divisions of Moto X and the X Games, he won Silver and Gold medals, respectively. With the formation of his company, Bioadapt, he builds and sells a variety of tough prosthetics that can withstand the demands of extreme sports.

Gregg returned from Afghanistan to his home in the United Kingdom as a double amputee. His extraordinary prosthetic limb has a Bluetooth remote control to switch from different action modalities such as walking, jogging, cycling, or golfing. It has amazing features such as being able to automatically sense and react to his movements and being waterproof (think shower or beach). Recently, he received a new £70,000 Genium X model knee that is programmed from a laptop and also uses Wii-style sensors to anticipate his action and adapts appropriately as a human leg would.

To be clear, these prosthetic limbs are not mass manufactured. They are elegantly customized to the user with sophisticated instruments and calibrated with extreme accuracy. To engineer a fit, the amputated limb extension is measured externally for its physicality, and imaging of the neuromuscular interior is assessed for the best support design. And then there is the assessment of the height and size of the user as well as specific needs. In the case of Adrianne, a dancer's movement was studied so the foot prosthetic can move fluidly with the ankle to allow for unusual movement. As a mountain climber, Dr. Herr has enjoyed the benefit of using different prosthetic feet to climb different terrain.

Bionics are making profound differences in people's lives. They are bringing ability to lives that were previously disabled and shining a bright light for a fulfilled future where there were only dim thoughts. Going forward, wearing exoskeletons will not be relegated to bionic needs, but will also become universally adapted as an advantage for the able-bodied. We are building a future of transparent adaptive technology for everyone.

"Innovative Technology Revolutionizes Prosthetic Legs" originally appeared on February 28, 2014 at *http://agingandcreativity.blogspot.com/2014/02/innovative-medical-technology-supports.html*.

The Evolving Wheelchair: Innovation, Adaptability, and Design

Money cannot buy health, but I'd settle for a diamond studded wheelchair.

Dorothy Parker

True or False:

1. All wheelchairs look alike
2. All wheelchairs have a grey or dark colored surface
3. All wheelchairs cost only a small fraction of the cost of a car
4. No wheelchair can climb stairs
5. Wheelchairs can never be used on sand, mud, or other exceptional terrain

The answer to all of the above is FALSE.

Wheelchairs have come a long way since their first debut in 1595 as an "invalid's chair" for Phillip II of Spain. Recently, industrial designers worldwide have taken the challenge to create the exceptional merger of form, function, and uniqueness.[33] Each has a different perspective on style, an approach to challenge the function, and a dazzling feature. Some prototypes are so unusual that they may never get to market or, if they did, they may not be able to sell enough wheelchairs to sustain their business. Yet wild designs are important because they break down the stereotypes, and then innovative elements start to appear in other models. Also the reverse is true. Seeing the capability of a wheelchair in a special way can trigger thoughts of advancing that feature with more functionality in a new model.

One of the most remarkable wheelchair innovations is a submersible model. British artist Sue Austin, a wheelchair user since 1996, pursued this development with a team of engineers. Adaptable for scuba diving, it uses dive thrusters, control surfaces, and flotation as well as fins attached to Sue's feet to propel underwater. Engaged in performance art, the wheelchair is part of her Freewheeling project, which addresses the intersection of art and disability.[34]

All-terrain wheelchairs are attracting interest. From moving gracefully on a sandy beach to climbing up and down stairs, these wheelchairs have been designed with unique sets of wheels. HEROes Series of Sport Wheelchairs inspired by Mark Zupan, a quadriplegic and captain of the United States wheelchair rugby team, built a wheelchair not just for the beach but predictably also for beach rugby. And a team of designers, Julia Kaisinger, Mathias Mayrhofer, and Benesch Xiulian, worked together to develop the Carrier Robotic Wheelchair that can provide complete independence for the user traveling over any terrain.[35] Its functions include traction to climb the stairs and a standing position so the user can be at eye level with other people and have the potential to reach things that previously could not be reached from a seated position. Another very special practical design element would eliminate the need to physically transfer to a toilet seat.

And there is the social and psychological aspect of being in a wheelchair that the average mobile person does not think about. Yet for Alexandre Pain, his design goal was "Designing for Social Stigma," and he wanted to create change with a dramatic and elegant design that does not resemble a wheelchair. To fully understand the dynamics of a wheelchair with respect to both its function and challenges of the user, he dedicated time being in the wheelchair. Alexandre found that the most difficult aspect was the stigma associated with it, and so his goal was to reinvent it, morph it into an entity that did not resemble its former life. The result is the electric Tandem scooter which is quite beautiful and, like a scooter, comes with additional seating for another person in the back. His goal is achieved with this reconceptualization because it reduces the negative perception of disability that is associated with a wheelchair.

More evolutionary wheelchair designs include:

The Nimbl concept wheelchair by designer Lawrence Kwok (with Tino Sacino, Danna Lei, and Alison Ochoa) enables the user to move through interior home space without having to make costly physical changes to the space.

The Firefly from Rio Mobility is an attachable electric handcycle. From the wheelchair position, a person can attach this device to the front. It transforms the wheelchair to a motorbike look and gives the user control with steering and speed.

The Cursum stroller for wheelchair users by designer Cindy Sjöblom greatly assists disabled parents. "Parenting in the first stages of infancy can be incredibly challenging—add a mobile disability to the equation, and you can imagine how daunting it might seem." This wheelchair was created to work in tandem with an infant seat.

Mauricio Maeda designed an entertainment mobile for the wheelchair user. "In my humble opinion, design should not be just about making beautiful things, but to improve people's lives and serve a purpose as well," Maeda said. "I decided to model a wheelchair because I hardly ever could find one that presented a little more comfort and some additional features (at least here in Japan!). I've put a portable computer case under the seat, a joystick (to move the wheelchair), a trackball, a monitor, a keyboard, speakers, a wireless headset, a webcam, a drink holder, a stereo sound gadget (behind the seat), a power source on the back and a remote control. Some other features could be added, but I didn't want to turn it into a Christmas tree. So that's it..."

There will always be people with disabilities. There will always be wheelchairs, but now designers have taken the challenge to blend form and function. Leaving the classic stereotype behind has given designers the freedom to bring more versatility to the wheelchair, and therefore, an enhanced quality of life to the user. For the disabled, it will provide more mobility and independence, and positively impact their social interactions, their options for leisure time, and their self-esteem.

"The Evolving Wheelchair: Innovation, Adaptability, and Design" originally appeared on February 28, 2013 at *http://agingandcreativity.blogspot. com/2013/02/the-evolving-wheelchair-innovation. html*. This article won a National Mature Media Award.

Octogenarians Create Fashion History

Fashion is not something that exists in dresses only. Fashion is in the sky, in the street, fashion has to do with ideas, the way we live, what is happening.

Coco Chanel

Hot pants. Bell bottoms. Miniskirts. Long skirts. Hand knits. Flat knits. Real fur. Faux fur. The fashion world is always changing. It starts with runway models strutting down the walk with very expensive clothes cut for their very thin bodies. It is fashion as art, not fashion as wearables for the masses. Still, there is a trickle down factor when these pieces are economically replicated or "knocked off" (as the garment trade refers to them) and sold in a range of sizes to women eagerly waiting for their inner fashionista to be sated.

But there is also a writhing pulse of extraordinary fashion right on the street. New York City streets.

Bill Cunningham built his career capturing the

wild and wonderful, the sublime and the ridiculous—people in their everyday lives wearing the extraordinary. His blue eyes are trained to spot the exceptional, and he quickly shoots the photos that are later posted in the Style section of *The New York Times*. At 82 years old, he weaves his way in and out of traffic, bicycling around Manhattan to galas, events, fashion shows, and parties. However, he is notably positioned at the corner of 57th Street and 5th Avenue, watching and snapping candid yet legendary photos that are visual statements of both fashion bravado and wearable art. "It isn't what I think, it's what I see," Mr. Cunningham says. "I let the street speak to me. You've got to stay on the street and let the street tell you what it is."

Just released, *Bill Cunningham New York* is a brilliant 88-minute documentary that captures the essence of Bill's stunning and singular career.[36] Directed by Richard Press, it is a unique gift to those who wish to relish the success of eccentricity and talent.

It takes a combination of artful passion and courage to create fashion as a visual expression without attention to the buying audience. Fashion companies approach it in reverse. But Roberto Capucci is a brilliant and talented renegade and, at age 82, he has sustained his vision his way to achieve enormous success.

The first US compilation of his work featuring over eighty pieces as well as drawings is now at the Philadelphia Museum of Art and titled *Roberto Capucci: Art Into Fashion*.[37] Capucci synergizes fabric, form, color, and texture to sculpt the body silhouette. With an artist's vision and an architect's mind, he folds, layers, and pleats fabric to create magical and unforgettable dress forms. In fact, a woman choosing to purchase a piece from his collection (there is no duplication or alterations) must fit into it and realize that, when worn, she is a secondary element to her three-dimensional fabric art. The movement generated by wearing a Capucci enhances its allure in space; all rotations spin different views as it gracefully moves and turns with the wearer. Although he also designs daywear as well as accessories such as shoes and perfume, it was his museum quality costumes that have earned him the Medal of Gold of Venice at age 26 and led to designing one-of-a-kind dresses for the most influential and affluent Europeans as well as American movie stars such as Marilyn Monroe and Gloria Swanson. "Having been a student of fine arts, I perhaps ended up in fashion by mistake," says Capucci. "My dresses belong more to the art world than the world of fashion, but this has been my destiny."

Sometimes we can change our destiny. Judith

Leiber was living in Nazi-occupied Budapest and instead of being exterminated because she was Jewish, she became a survivor by escaping with her family to Switzerland. Right after the war, she met and married an American soldier, Gerson Leiber, and they moved to the United States in 1948. After working for various handbag companies, she started her own business in 1963 with Gerson's help. Now her spectacular handbags are one of the most sought after luxury brands and an elite status symbol owned by royalty, celebrities, and First Ladies.[38] Beverly Sills, the opera singer, was known to have a collection of almost 200 Leiber purses. All of these artful handbags are meticulously crafted and beautifully styled. Leiber is well known for her minaudieres, which are usually covered in crystals. Some with an animal theme can cost in excess of $5000. Recognized for her iconic work with numerous awards, she remarks, "I was the first woman to receive a Coty Award, and it was the first time it had been given to anyone for a handbag." Her unique purse designs are on permanent display at the Smithsonian in Washington, DC, the Metropolitan Museum of Art in New York City, the Victoria and Albert Museum in London, and in their own Leiber Collection museum in East Hampton (established in 2005), which showcases hundreds of her handbags in addition to her husband's art and their unique collection of Chinese porcelains.

In 1993, Judith sold her business to a London-based company. She says, "Half the success of a business is luck, and the other half is talent, and I managed to put that together, so we were very fortunate." Now at age 89, she owns about 900 of her own bags, although she created approximately 3500 different styles and says, "We would love to have them all."

All three of these talented octogenarians have sustained a long career in making fashion interesting and important. Their legacy lies in their devotion to their art form, their approach to making their work accessible, and their vision that propels them forward so history can be captured again and again.

"Octogenarians Create Fashion History" originally appeared as "Three Creative Octogenarians Create Fashion History" on April 5, 2011 at *http://agingandcreativity.blogspot.com/2011/04/octogenarians-create-fashion-history.html.*

Three Holocaust Survivors and Their Creative Success

We shall draw from the heart of suffering itself
the means of inspiration and survival.

Winston Churchill

World War II ended almost seventy years ago, but the impact of the Holocaust still lives with over 200,000 survivors worldwide. Although it is difficult to accurately capture exact data on the number of survivors, it is estimated that their average age is 79 years old. Although so many brilliant and talented individuals were killed in camps, fortunately there are individuals who are alive and have experienced successful creative lives despite incredible obstacles.

The following is a brief outline of three successfully creative Holocaust survivors:

Samuel Bak, 81: Painter and Writer

An exceptional artist, who some acknowledge to be the greatest living painter of the Holocaust, Bak has developed his art from a young age. He was born in Lithuania/Poland where, at the age of 9 years old, he had his first exhibition inside the confines of the Vilna Ghetto. Survived with only his mother, after the war they eventually settled in Israel, where he studied art at the Bezalel Academy of Arts and Design in Jerusalem.

A collection of Bak's works is on permanent display at Pucker Gallery in Boston, Massachusetts, and many exhibitions of his art have been in prominent museums and galleries worldwide.

- 2001 Publication of his book *Painted in Words: A Memoir* (printed in four languages)
- 2002 Received the Herkomer Cultural Prize in Landsberg, Germany

Judith (Peto) Leiber, 93: Handbag designer

Born in Hungary, Judith was preparing for university matriculation in London when she returned home to be with her family despite the new restrictions for Jews. "Hitler put me in the handbag business," Judith says, because Jews were not allowed to study, so she had to learn a trade. Met and married Gerson (Gus) Leiber, an American GI, in Budapest, and they settled in New York City. She worked for various handbag companies when, in the 1960s, with encouragement from her husband, she began her own company. Judith Leiber's worldwide success is an extraordinary story of hard work, smarts, and enormous technical and visual talent. Her handbags are on permanent display at the Smithsonian in Washington, DC; the Metropolitan Museum of Art in New York City; the Victoria and Albert Museum in London; and her own museum, The Leiber Collection, in East Hampton, New York.

- 1973 Coty American Fashion Critics Award
- 1980 Silver Slipper Award from the Costume Institute of the Museum of Fine Arts in Houston
- 1994 Lifetime Achievement Award from the Council of Fashion Designers of America
- 2010 Visionary Woman Award from Moore College of Art & Design

Yoram Gross, 87: Animation artist of stories for children

Born in Poland, he loved music above all and says, "All I wanted to do was play Chopin." He and his family were on Oskar Schindler's famous list, but they decided to take their own risk to escape by moving and hiding in places seventy-two times. He later moved to Israel, where he worked and learned about documentaries and films and then moved to Australia where, with his wife, he honed his animation skills and created experimental films. Well known for his series of *Blinky Bill* and *Dot and the Kangaroo*, he tells stories to the hearts of children that are rooted in the Holocaust experience and laced with lessons of survival, kindness, and triumph.

- 80+ international awards for various films
- 1995 Order of Australia
- 2011 Autobiography, *My Animated Life*

The University of Southern California's Shoah Foundation and the University's Institute for Creative Technologies are working on an extraordinary project to create holographic interviews available at museums worldwide. Designed to be an interactive exhibit, it will inform, educate, and create a permanent remembrance for many, many years. After the remaining Holocaust survivors have passed on, their legacies will remain visible and audible in perpetuity. The lessons should never be forgotten.

"Three Holocaust Survivors and Their Creative Success" originally appeared on January 31, 2014 at *http://agingandcreativity.blogspot.com/2014/01/ two-living-holocaust-survivors-and.html*.

Apfel at Age 90: More is More and Less is Simply Less

You only have one trip (one life) so you might as well enjoy it.

Iris Apfel

In order to be irreplaceable one must always be different.

Coco Chanel

Forget the old saying "Less is More." Minimalists thrived on that belief because it validated their art, but the contemporary fashion niche embraced by Iris Apfel makes a different statement.[39] Turn your head 180 degrees and open your eyes wide and your mind even wider. There she is—a fashion maverick, an irreverent renegade, a defiant creative spirit, and a marvel of an exquisite opulence of wearables.

"I'm a geriatric starlet, my dear, don't you know," she said. "All of a sudden, I'm hot; I'm cool; I have a 'fan base'."

With a rising cult of diverse people spilling around her amazing presence, Apfel is taking her show on the road. The HSN road, that is. Middle America is fascinated and wants this design eccentricity to be a brand in their lives. Naturally, much will be in translation. For example, her classic owl-shape eyeglasses will be featured in a scarf print, and tribal-type necklaces are modified with respect to design and price.

Iris was always a fashion maven. "My mother worshipped at the altar of accessories, and I got the bug. She always said, if you have a good, little, simple black dress and you have different accessories, you can have 27 different outfits." So she learned early. "The fun of getting dressed is that it is a creative experience, and I never know what it's going to be." She assiduously edits her ensembles, often wearing a basic architectural type of garment that can be accessorized dramatically. In 2005, the Metropolitan Museum of Art in New York City presented an exhibition about Apfel called *Rara Avis (Rare Bird): The Irreverent Iris Apfel*. It was so successful that they created a traveling version that could be viewed by other audiences.

"Composing the elements of interior and composing an ensemble are part and parcel of the same thought process," says Apfel. So she was a natural, watching her father in his business working with high-end mirrors that focused on interiors. This passion for interiors catapulted the careers of Iris and her husband, Carl. Serendipitously, they started working with Old World Weavers in search of a certain cloth and then began to travel worldwide looking for both exotic fabrics and historically based designs that could be replicated by foreign specialty mills. It was through this work that she was asked to consult for the White House interior for Presidents Truman, Eisenhower, Nixon, Kennedy, Johnson, Carter, Reagan, and Clinton.

Married sixty-four years, Apfel and her almost 100 year old husband wear the same perfume called *Yatagan* by Caron, which is hard to find, so they store it in big containers in the refrigerator. They also wear similar round spectacles. An amazing couple, they have been very successful in their fabric business; despite retirement from Old World Weavers in the 1990s, it's clear that Iris's fame is soaring. This radical fashion icon will be featured in an upcoming documentary by Albert Maysles while she continues to design products for various companies and has the magnanimous vision to donate more than 900 pieces from her wardrobe to the Peabody Essex Museum in Salem, Massachusetts.

Iris Apfel is an iconic legend with the bravado and mastery of greatness.

"Apfel at Age 90: More is More and Less is Simply Less" originally appeared May 31, 2012 at *http:// agingandcreativity.blogspot.com/2012/05/apfel-at-age-90-more-is-more-and-less.html.*

Reinventing Embroidery: Experimental and Extraordinary Art

Art is the most intense mode of individualism that the world has known.

Oscar Wilde

I don't paint things. I only paint the difference between things.

Henri Matisse

New work has emerged that has revolutionized the concept of embroidery as a traditional handcraft. Gone are those little blue "x"s printed on cloth for following an embroidery pattern. These new artists have transformed the basic concept of this craft and have elevated it to an exceptional art form.

Shizuko Kimura is 75 years old.[40] Born in Japan, she studied painting and then received a degree in textiles from the Royal College of Art in London. She uses thread like a pencil to explore the human form and create portraits that are both exquisite in detail organized creative process. The book contains seven short essays that describe the discovery and essence of that process. The projects in the book then illustrate it and offer what I call "what if...?s," suggestions for taking the original designs in new and exciting directions. I truly believe that anyone who truly wants to be creative and is willing to do the work, can be. Giving yourself permission to BELIEVE that you CAN be creative is often half the battle.

Zausner Your beaded knit work is extraordinary and basically singular in availability. Are they all singular pieces, or do you ever produce, contract production or consider alternatives for demand of multiple pieces?

Hershberg I make every single piece I sell, so the idea of doing production for large-scale retail sale is not possible, nor do I have any interest in doing that. Perhaps selfishly, I want to make only what I want to make, when I want to make it. But, in addition to my more costly, one-of-a-kind work, I do have a line of limited edition pieces: what I call Slider Bracelets and Bead Ball Necklaces. These are still made to order but simpler and quite affordable, ranging in price from $75 per bead ball to $125 for a bracelet. In the past, I have only sold my work at shows or from my studio showroom by appointment, but that is about to change. Sometime in the next few months

I will be adding an e-commerce component to my website where people will be able to directly order my limited edition work and buy an occasional sale piece of one-of-a-kind work as well as a new line of original pattern designs and accompanying material kits. When the new Studio B Shop site *(http://www.studiobknits.com/)* launches, I'll announce it on my website and on Ravelry.

Zausner You manage many avenues of generating Betsy Hershberg excitement: teaching, pattern making, book writing, kit making, and of course your own knit projects. Do you enjoy working with all of these entities?

Hershberg While I really do enjoy teaching and writing, the book was an incredible experience (made possible by the extraordinary publishing team at XRX Books with whom I had the privilege of working), there is no question that imagining and creating new, one-of-a-kind work is my absolute favorite endeavor. The process I use often involves the iterative creation of small, ever-evolving swatches as I shepherd an idea from whatever inspiration is at play to a finished piece. The work is challenging, exciting, and yet, because it happens in small steps, it never feels scary or overwhelming. Perfect for a somewhat risk-averse, left-brainer like me.

Zausner At 63, you have achieved tremendous success with your work and your teaching both in person and through your book. Do you have a further vision for yourself? An area yet untapped?

Hershberg Not really. I much prefer to remain open to whatever life will offer up next. I am never bored! The word does not exist in my vocabulary. Given my past, I have every reason to expect that the next adventure will be as much fun and rewarding as those that I've already experienced. I am an eternal optimist, another gift I have "inherited" from my remarkable mother—now a healthy, actively engaged, 87 year old. Whatever awaits, I am confident I'll find a way to deal with the challenges and celebrate the joys.

This interview with Betsy Hershberg originally appeared on June 16, 2013 at *http://agingandcreativity.blogspot.com/2013/06/an-interview-with-betsy-hershberg.html.*

Ed Bing Lee
Never Not Knotting Fiber

Photo © Ken Yanoviak

As a child of Chinese immigrants, Ed has taken his craft to the art world. He creates hand-knotted, small artful objects, and the series, Delectable, *is a charming and beautifully crafted replication of American junk food.*

Zausner As a child of Chinese immigrants whose father died young, and your mother worked in a sewing factory, your roots were humble. You were fortunately recognized for your artistic talent in grade school and later went on to earn two Master degrees and become a successful fiber artist. Do you reflect on your achievement and the roads that paved the path to where you are now?

Lee As I look back on the fifty-odd years of working in the "arts," the experience has afforded me with much pleasure, some surprises, few disappointments, and even regrets. One regret is that I never took the time to explore large-scale knotted pieces, a point of view undergoing revision in my current work as well as in future projects.

Zausner Your creative experience using knotting began around 1970 while you were teaching off loom techniques. What you say about knotting is that "you can go two-dimensional, three-dimensional, or you can do both at the same time. And there's no machinery." Certainly knotting does not require any machinery, and it does not require tools either. Since it is relegated to your hands only, do you treat your hands with special creams, gloves, or exercises to keep them nimble and able to handle all your creative ideas?

Lee I have been fortunate in that I have not experienced any extreme trauma with the use of my hands. I don't have any special routine for their care. Of late I try to minimize any straining motions and have slowed my pace considerably. Mostly, I rest frequently and try to vary hand actions so that I'm not repeating the same motion endlessly.

Zausner Is all your work entirely fiber? That is to say, you primarily work with waxed linen, embroidery floss and synthetic ribbons although you have included paper and shoelaces in your *Chawan* series. Do you often explore using other linear or fibrous elements, or is your focus primarily on the form and the process?

Lee Linen and embroidery floss were the only materials I used when I started knotting. The two dimensional pieces, as in the *Picnic* series, and as in the art history-inspired figural pieces, were made exclusively in these two materials. The warp was linen and embroidery floss and served to create the pictorial images, all in an effort to simulate a tapestry.

I started using waxed linen in my *Earthcrust* series because it allowed me to incorporate three-dimensional projections as in a bas-relief. The structural character of the waxed linen also facilitated the making of freestanding sculptural images which I combined with the richer palette of the embroidery floss, the wellspring of the *Delectable* series.

The *Chawan* series was a period of learning and experimentation for me. I started to use new materials: ribbons, shoelaces, costume trimming, paper cords, and ribbons. More importantly, I started to use a wider variety of knots and combined materials of different weights and textures within a single piece. To date *Chawan* was my largest series numbering some fifty items.

Zausner In developing your art, you appear to have launched yourself from your knowledge as a painter and skill as a fiber architect. By interpreting the pointillism of Seurat, you created a knotted translation. In your *Delectable* series, your work is an interpretation of popular iconic American foods. Each one is a series to build upon and consider. Are you currently working on another thematic project?

Lee Currently I'm considering two distinct series. In the works are large sculptural pieces which contain aspects from the *Delectable* series. The treatment is more abstract. The form, color, and texture of the images in the *Delectable* relied heavily on their actual counterparts. But in the new food series, I'm trying to center my attention on the elements of design and composition. I would like these new pieces to have a presence as Art independent of their source.

The second series exists mostly in my imagination, but I am beginning to see definable outlines. Possibly a series of miniatures combining art historical and contemporary images within a single pictorial format.

Zausner In the process of creating a new piece, do you plan for it by rendering sketches? If so, do you include structural elements?

Lee As a preface to this question, the actual making of a knotted object is a long (emphasize long) process. Several months is not out of the question, and a few select pieces require a more substantial block of time. My process is to picture the finished piece in my mind; consider the construction (materials, size, color, and most importantly, the starting point); followed by visualizations in drawings with appropriate remarks and notations; then start knotting. It is very rare that the completed piece is like what I had imagined. A large part of the cause for rethink and adjustments is precipitated by the fact that all my sculptural pieces are hollow, which affects the design, the type of material, and certainly the construction. A case in point: I like my pieces to be self-supporting, which may entail reinforcing the walls.

Common practice for most sculptural knotters is to use a supporting form around which they knot. When finished, the support would be completely covered. This practice renders a much smoother and uniform surface.

Zausner You were honored to receive the Pew Fellowships in the Arts award, have exhibited widely, and your art is in esteemed collections. Does this success fuel your creative energy?

Lee This question gave me a pause. All too often

achievements are measured as a linear unfolding, as one milestone after another. However, I feel the term "achievement" is bit too formal for me, preferring to think of the different stages as beads of different sizes, significances, and magnitude of importance being strung together, representing the whole of my work while I continue to add beads. The following lines by Rudyard Kipling in his poem, "If—," capture my sentiments very succinctly:

> *"If you can meet with Triumph and Disaster*
> *And treat those two impostors just the same..."*

Zausner You say that "challenge moves my work forward." You have certainly used challenge to move your life forward. Now at eighty, what creative challenge lies ahead?

Lee I believe that what I have done in the past is an integral part of what I am doing now. When starting a new series, I seek to present these selfsame "borrowings" in a different light. It is a process of deconstructing and revitalizing my artistic vision.

Another aspect that I would like to see embodied in my work is what has been described by Hanneke Grootenboer in his *The Rhetoric of Perspective*—that Art is capable of presenting complex thoughts that are often contradictory, so Art can represent "thinking in a way that is superficial and profound, empty and meaningful, playful and serious." Finally, I would like to have enough work for a solo in my mid 80s. Is it possible to have it all?

This interview with Ed Bing Lee originally appeared on August 9, 2013 at *http://agingandcreativity. blogspot.com/2013/08/an-interview-with-ed-bing-lee-never-not.html.*

Tim Lefens
Painter, Art Activist

Tim Lefens has opened a new world for the severely physically challenged. As Founder and Executive Director of A.R.T. (Artistic Realization Technologies), Lefens has pioneered new ways for this population to express themselves creatively through art. He has cognitively freed them and watched their self-esteem and sense of purpose blossom. Media has noticed and picked up this terrific story, and Lefen's own book, Flying Colors, *is a testament to the power of his work. Lefens has been blind for years, but at fifty-seven his passion and dedication to the A.R.T. mission remain at full throttle.*

Zausner Before you started A.R.T., you were actively involved in your own art as a painter. Did you have formal education and/or training in art? Can you talk about your art now?

Lefens Yes, I went to art school and had a long string of great mentors including Roy Lichtenstein, Clement Greenberg, and Jules Olitski. These were great artists who adopted me and helped tune in my understanding of art.

I continue to paint and show in New Jersey galleries. I've almost always been close to monochrome even when I had 20/20 vision. Also, I have never really been into color, but more focused on drawing and tactility. By just using your hands and imagination, you can feel the shape of the painting and know where you're placing the built up paint. When it comes time to add color, I simply talk to someone to get the color I want.

Zausner What areas of the creative process does A.R.T. address? How are the components designed?

Lefens There is Painting, Sculpture, Music Composition, and Photography. Painting is the least technical area because it only uses a laser; it's a core basic program and the least expensive. The Music program works with our light actuated synthesizer with light sensitive diodes and costs thousands of dollars.

By interacting directly with an A.R.T. artist, I get ideas of how things should be done technically, for example, how the sculpture should move, how they can select the music notes. And I think about how that can be done with power. I have been fortunate to find engineers who have offered their services at very modest fees and have been able to develop the device. There are no patents for these devices; there are only prototypes and they have never been replicated.

Zausner Your A.R.T. program involves recruiting physically challenged people to participate in the creative process, seeking financial sponsorships, and harnessing technology. Where are the greatest challenges?

Lefens After about seventeen years of being on the road, our biggest challenge is in the perception of the able-bodied. We manage to get some funding to keep going and have solved the problems of the population we are serving. However, our challenge is not the quadriplegic non-verbal people; the challenge is how they are seen by the able-bodied. So we are always working on this. If the physically challenged are thought of as incapable, then they are treated as incapable, and there is no way out.

Zausner Your book, *Flying Colors,* talks about your

personal and professional journey with A.R.T. Is there other media, such as a documentary, in development?

Lefens There is a documentary that was just finished, and there will be a screening in July [2011]. You can see a trailer at *http://decemberart.com.* Also, the book has now been translated into Chinese.

Zausner The A.R.T. program is now running in multiple locations around the country. Can you talk about that?

Lefens There are about twenty-seven fully functional satellites including the UK, Canada, and New Zealand. Once we saw the breakthrough in 1994, and how easy it works and how profoundly effective, we had a goal to be global. Our first trip was to California, and then we went to New Mexico, Florida, Tennessee, Massachusetts, Pennsylvania, and Ohio. We will go anywhere we can. Some of these states have multiple sites. For example, in Florida, we have seven sites, in Pennsylvania there are two, Ohio has one. Each state is different.

We want the people running the sites to bond with us so we can provide guidance. Those who have realized that benefit have succeeded big time especially since talking to us does not cost them.

The sites sell paintings to help fund their programs but they also need grants. For exhibitions, I urge them to aim high; to have a show in a museum rather than a café. Art shows tend to move people who have the capacity to fund, and successful examples are Little Rock, Arkansas, and Jacksonville, Florida, which are selling hundreds of paintings. At both sites, we are in touch weekly.

For new sites, they find us or we find them. Then we assess their situation; they need a minimum of five people to launch the A.R.T. program. After months of pre-education, once they're ready we fly out. Then, after we do the workshops on site, it is not unusual to hear the staff sobbing and leaving the room because they have been working with these people forever, and now all of a sudden they're alive. It's very intense.

Zausner In A.R.T. exhibitions, some artists sell their work for substantial sums of money. How are they priced? Do you court collectors?

Lefens Pricing is tricky and basically it is what the market will bear. A high selling mark is about $2400. Our collectors include a former governor and other serious buyers. One collector, a marine supply company, has purchased over seventy paintings from our Jacksonville site to fill their offices at corporate headquarters. Then once they were filled, they started shipping art pieces to their sister headquarters in the Netherlands. Now they are moving to Houston so we hope to open that market.

Zausner You have suffered with a vision problem and are now totally blind. This must be an extraordinary challenge for you to manage your work. How long had it been progressing, and how do you manage A.R.T.?

Lefens They don't really know what the condition is, but have labeled it retinitis pigmentosa. I was diagnosed in 1988 and had no visual aids. However, the miracle was the talking computer, because I wrote the entire *Flying Colors* book without a computer screen, and not a word was changed by my publisher. Window-Eyes was the software I used to write; it was very fast and the editor did not change one word.

I do not accommodate or embrace my condition. I do not deny that I am blind, but I do deny its presence. I also work in an absorption mode, which is when you have something so fascinating in your life that it displaces thoughts of having a disability. So my approach is a unique combination of denial and absorption.

Zausner In a perfect world, what would you imagine for A.R.T. ?

Lefens That A.R.T. will be universally accepted and embraced. That we give the population that we work with and love not only respect, joy, and freedom, but also that it would wake up the able-bodied. Everyone would realize that you cannot judge a person from the outside. Period.

This interview with Tim Lefens originally appeared on May 30, 2011 at *http://agingandcreativity.blogspot.com/2011/05/interview-with-tim-lefens-painter-art.html.*

Judith Leiber
From Survivor to Artisan to Fashion Icon

Photo © Sandra Wong Geroux

As a young Hungarian immigrant, Judith brought her skills, tools, and passion for making handbags. Now over a half-century later, her extraordinary handbags are in the collections of the Metropolitan Museum of Art, The Smithsonian Institution, The Victoria and Albert Museum, and also in her and her husband's unique museum on Long Island.

Zausner In Hungary, as a young adult during World War II, you and your family struggled to stay alive. Now many decades later, you have achieved remarkable success both professionally through your business and personally with a marriage spanning more than sixty years. Do you reflect on those very difficult years and your life journey?

Leiber I try not to think about those days because it was really very difficult. And I try, what we went through so much in five years of war, but we are happy that we got over that and achieved success in the handbag business.

Zausner Since Jews were forbidden to study in a Hungarian university and you could not return to King's College in London where you had just begun studies, you stayed in Budapest to be with your family and learn a trade. You said, "Hitler put me in the handbag business," and so your career started in Hungary. Can you imagine that your creativity, drive, and technical acumen could have been channeled successfully at that time in a different profession?

Leiber Yes, Jews were forbidden to study in Hungarian University. And so my parents sent me to King's College in London to learn chemistry with the thought that I would work in cosmetics, because I had an aunt and uncle in Romania who made an enormous success with a cream called Flora Cream.

But funnily enough, I never got to really study at King's College. I just passed the matriculation and then returned to Hungary in the summer so that I wouldn't waste my father's money for the time that I wasn't there. I never returned to England because of the war.

Zausner You created a vast collection of the most

exceptional and artful handbags over many decades. Growing up did you realize that you had a creative flair? An entrepreneurial soul? Were you interested in fashion?

Leiber Well, I had a creative flair, I suppose, but I didn't really know anything about business, although my dad had been in business all his life. He worked for a big bank and was very successful there. And he taught me how to handle things whenever you get into business; what you have to do in order to make a profit. I learned that from him.

I always liked fashion, but in Hungary there weren't that many things that you could worry about with that. My sister and I had two Lenci dolls that my parents got us in Italy. And, when we were little, we even had paintings of each one of the dolls. They were both girl dolls, and they were just wonderful. But after what happened during the war, either they got lost, or we never worried about it after that. You didn't have the time to worry about things like that.

When I came to the United States, I was, of course, very interested in what people were doing in the clothing business. In the very beginning, I made bags right away that I thought would be successful to wear with clothes. That was very fortunate.

Zausner You worked for different handbag companies until your husband, Gus, persuaded you to open your own business in 1963. Presidential First Ladies and royalty have enjoyed wearing your bags as a fashion statement of status.

Leiber I worked for the most expensive handbag company. When I went there, I went to the head of the pocketbook makers' union, and I said to the guy, "Whatever, you'll send me up there, you'll see." He said, "You're not going to make it." But, you know, I thought, well, if they send me there, I'm going to stick there. I'll be all right. And they had a pattern maker, a sample maker, who was the head of it. And I was his assistant when I got there. But after a while, he got very sick and couldn't work anymore, and they gave me the job. So I was doing everything. First, I was just making all the patterns and the pieces. And then, I even ran the floor at the end.

I worked there until 1960. Then I went to work for Morris Moskowitz for a couple of years. And my husband said, "You're not going to work for these schnooks anymore. You are, we are, going into business." Of course, I was scared to death, and we were scared to death about every problem that we ever had. But, on the other hand, we made some wonderful bags, so we were a big success. It was a small business, but we were very fortunate. It took a lot of work, but we did it. We worked very hard.

I also used a lot of antique frames that I copied and made animal bags: dogs, cats, bears, and many shapes that were just somewhat classical. And I made a very wonderful Tiffany-style bag from one of the Tiffany windows in the Met and some other little bags that were also based on Tiffany which were very nice looking. One of the original Tiffany bags that I made was for Laura Bush for her second inaugural. The Pop Art I did was very successful; we sold a lot of them.

Zausner Which handbags or styles are you particularly happy with and do you wear them?

Leiber One of my favorite bags is a *chatelaine*. It's a little purse shape, which started me on making bags with rhinestones in 1967. It's still my favorite because it put me into the rhinestone business.

I have a very small collection at this point, but, you know, if I ever wanted to wear a bag, we have a lot of bags upstairs. We keep bags in cases very nicely put away, and I could always borrow one of my bags from the collection if I wanted to wear it.

Zausner Your bags span a vast range of extraordinary styles in elegant materials from leather to satin to metal (and rhinestone-based) and a unique range of styles from classic to formal to Pop Art. Which designs have been the most challenging to implement?

Leiber I was very fortunate that Gus brought me here. I was very lucky. Anyway, every design I ever made I started with an idea and then made all the patterns for them. I used all leathers: alligator, lizard, snake, calf, suede, satin, oriental, obis, Indian ribbons from Mumbai. The Indians had these black robes that had colorful borders and we bought those borders. And we put the silk or leather in between each ribbon and made it up like that. They were absolutely wonderful after we finished them.

When I started out, we had four people. Then we got a little bigger and had thirty-two workers in the factory. After 1967, we started to make fully beaded bags, not just the one that was originally done. I had a man who used to do the rhinestones for us, and when that company went out of business, I took the best girl they had, and she taught a lot of the other girls how to work on things like that. We taught them how to do the beading and it worked out very well. We had one hundred girls just doing beadwork.

Zausner Were you ever interested in designing for men?

Leiber I never tried to do designs for men. I had my hands full with the handbags and the belts and the jewelry that I made.

Zausner Did you design costume jewelry or precious jewelry?

Leiber Yes, I had a small costume jewelry business when we started out, but I said to my husband that we don't earn any real money on it. We stopped making it, even though he felt we should have kept it up, but we didn't. Then Harry Winston's son, Ron Winston, came to see me, and said I should design real jewelry. So we did quite a bit in that, but once I sold the business, the man who bought it wanted the license. So we told him, "Fine, you use the license. It's yours."

Zausner Before selling your business and retiring in 1998, you received numerous prestigious awards and the Smithsonian, the Metropolitan Museum of Art, and other museums have your bags in their collections. Do you still design for your own pleasure?

Leiber I got a tremendous number of awards. My first award was the Swarovski Award, which was a little glass piece, very pretty. The Metropolitan Museum has eighty-eight of my bags, not all of them are from me. Some ladies gave them bags, too. And then I got the Coty Award in 1973, ten years after we were in business. And then in the last year that we owned the business, I had the CFDA Lifetime Achievement

Award. And I also got a Lifetime Achievement Award a few years before from the Accessories Business. And I had all kinds of other awards including a very beautiful award from Moore College.

Zausner You established the Leiber Collection museum in the East Hampton hamlet of Springs, New York, to primarily showcase your work and the art work of your husband. Has this new venture been an exciting chapter for you?

Leiber Six or seven years ago, my husband built a museum. He had a little help from an architect, but the bulk of the work, the ideas were all his. The building is sort of Palladian and looks very nice.

We are showing not just my handbags. There is a part of my work that is displayed permanently, but this year we also had a very large display of different kinds of bags, about 500, in the big room that usually is used for paintings.

It's really a great little building, and Gus is going to show some of his work next summer. He's working very hard this winter, making lots of paintings. He's also going to have a show at the Carter Burden Gallery, which only shows older artists who didn't have large success with their work in the market.

Zausner Now at age 92, having had a remarkably

long career, long marriage, long life, and having built a large estate, what dreams do you still have?

Leiber As far as the future is concerned, we are now hoping to live long enough to have a seventieth marriage anniversary. On February 5th (2014) we will be married sixty-eight years. We want to be able to enjoy our life and carry on for many more years. And once we go, this museum is going to be endowed enough so that it will go on for a long, long time after we are gone.

This interview with Judith Leiber originally appeared on November 20, 2013 at *http://agingand-creativity.blogspot.com/2013/11/an-interview-with-judith-leiber-from.html.*

Mitch Lyons
Artist, Printmaker, Founder of Clay Printing

Mitch Lyons is a very talented artist and also a pioneer. He developed a unique technique of creating two dimensional art using clay called clay printing. An inventor and a clay aficionado, he has mastered the elements of this process while, at 74 years old, he continues to explore more and more of its potential.

Photo © Carson Zullinger

Zausner When did you first start working in clay? Where was it? What type of art were you making prior to working with clay?

Lyons My artistic career started while I was a student at The University of the Arts in Philadelphia (previously called Philadelphia College of Art). While I was a printmaking major, sometime in my junior year, I wandered down to the basement where I witnessed magic. For the first time in my life I saw someone throwing on the potters' wheel, and as they say, it was love at first sight. I knew then and there that this is what I wanted to do for the rest of my life.

Zausner Can you describe the clay printing technique/process?

Lyons Printing with colored clay is a printing process that uses a slab of wet clay as the matrix, and china clay slip with organic pigments as the "ink." The slip is applied to the wet slab using a variety of techniques, i.e., slip trailing, stenciling, stamping, etc., to develop the design. A wooden rolling pin— "the press"—is rolled over a dampen paper that pulls a thin layer of colored clay from the matrix. Many monoprints can be pulled from the same slab without re-charging the slab.

Zausner How did you transition from classic 3D ceramics to 2D clay printing?

Lyons For me, and this has been true my whole artistic career, making clay prints and clay pots are the same. I never felt that I transitioned from 2D to 3D. All the techniques that I have developed over the last forty-five years are the same for either. If push came to shove, I will say that I am a potter making prints.

Zausner What was the evolution of your clay printing techniques over the years?

Lyons When I first started making clay prints in 1968, I was more structured in my thinking. First I thought that I needed an absorbent surface like paper to apply to the wet clay slab. For twelve years I experimented with paper (1968 to 1980) with some success. My images were also very structured and more conservative, less abstract. Around 1979 I found myself in a fabric store and noticed a roll of Pellon hanging from the ceiling. I inquired about it and was told that it was non-absorbent and figured it would not work for me. But I purchased a yard of it and went home and immediately stuck it in my print drawer and forgot about it. Probably about six months later I pulled it out and tried it. It worked, and worked much better than I had imagined. What was going on here? This experience was a pivotal change in my direction to develop clay printing. While researching this change, I discovered that Pellon, used by the clothing industry, has a slight static charge built into the fabric. This charge helps "pull" clay from the slab because clay also has a charge. One has a negative charge and one has a positive. All of this change slowly permeated my way of thinking more about the process than the product. This helped me get out of my comfort zone and try working "without a net." Many new ideas and changes occurred during this time, i.e., using pastels, transfers slips from paper, mark making using tools, and textures.

Zausner You use special paper for printing. Can you describe the properties that make it important?

Lyons After I discovered the benefits of Pellon, then I went to the internet to find out more about the static charge. This led me to the Non-Woven industry, which is not used for clothing, but for filtering, i.e., air conditioning, water, vacuum bags, coffee filters, and in 1985, Swiffer. The material that I have been using is called Reemay. It is primarily used for air conditioning and water filtering.

Zausner You teach these techniques in workshops all over the country and abroad. What is the response to your workshops?

Lyons For about thirty years I have been teaching clay printing all over the world. I have taught approximately 300 workshops since 1983 and probably over 2000 students. In addition, I have sold about 2000 copies of my DVD: *The Art of Clay Printing with Mitch Lyons*. On the internet, the search for clay monoprints finds about two dozen sites that show past students' work. Although there are not many clay printers out there, I always get positive results from students who take my workshop. Clay printing is still new to the art community. The word is spreading but very slowly. I think the response is great, and would like it to be far greater.

Zausner As an artist, do you have an upcoming exhibition? Are you in collections?

Lyons Currently I have an exhibition in the Old City Jewish Arts Center in Philadelphia, which ends this November (2012). Another exhibition is in Brad Smith's studio right after Thanksgiving, and for the first two weekends in December I will have my annual OPEN STUDIO, which will celebrate our twenty-seventh year.

My work can be found in many personal collections as well as some major museums. Brooklyn Museum of Art, Delaware Art Museum, Noyse Museum of Art, and also in university collections: University of Delaware, Bradley University, American University, and others.

Zausner What new techniques are you working with, and what is your vision for clay printing going forward?

Lyons Recently I have been experimenting with the computer to add digital images to my clay prints. I have also begun to print on various grades of sandpaper and play with the idea of using decals to apply to the clay print. After over forty years of printing with clay, I am still very excited about the technique.

I must say that I am blessed that I not only found a wonderful way of working, but it also perfectly fits my personality. Not sure where this will take me, but I am getting out of the way.

———

This interview with Mitch Lyons originally appeared on November 14, 2012 at *http://agingandcreativity. blogspot.com/2012/11/mitch-lyons-artist-founder- of-clay.html.*

Alice and Richard Matzkin
Painter and Sculptor

*Alice and Richard Matzkin,
painter and sculptor respectively,
are artists whose work focuses
on aging. Now in their 70s, they
express their thoughts about their
own aging and offer wise advice
for all of us.*

Photo © Sally Carless

Zausner Have you been actively engaged in making art your whole life?

Richard Matzkin In my early years, I was immersed in art but then completely lost interest in it as I began to pursue a career in music and psychology in the early 1960s. Then, twenty-five years later, my wife, Alice, enrolled me in a clay sculpture class. From the first day onward, I began to produce figurative sculptures with ease and without reference to models or photographs.

In my career I was a therapist, a men's group leader, Adjunct Instructor in the California Community College system, director of a court-mandated treatment program for domestic violence, and program director of a psychiatric hospital. I hold a Masters degree in Psychology.

Alice Matzkin I have received no formal education in art, but as long as I can remember, painting and drawing have been my love.

After a twenty-two year hiatus from painting, while I raised my son and daughter, I returned with passion to my paints and canvas. Since moving to the country with Richard, where we share a studio, I painted two paintings which were purchased —one of the famous potter and sculptor, Beatrice Wood at age 100, and feminist Betty Friedan—by the National Portrait Gallery of the Smithsonian Institution and are in their permanent collection.

Zausner Did something happen that provoked thoughts on your own aging?

Alice Matzkin I was about 58 years old when I began thinking of my mortality. I realized that part of coming to terms with the aging body is appreciating just how precious life is. And I also knew that if we didn't change our attitude about getting older we would be very unhappy.

Zausner How have you used your art to express your thoughts on aging?

Richard Matzkin Fear can be inspirational, and I sculpt my fears in clay. I began a series of "Naked Old Men," and I also worked on a series of old lovers which is all about us. My art helped me work through the issues of getting older. If you look at an old face without judgment, you see the person, the history, the character. And that has its own beauty but most people don't do that.

Zausner Alice, you have painted many older women, famous and not famous, naked and clothed. Is there something universal that you sense with all of these women?

Alice Matzkin I see how the body, although very different for each woman, is simply not what constitutes the person. It's inside that is important, living in the moment, accepting one's self. When we get older, we tend to compare ourselves with youthful beauty, but we're only young for a very short time, and each age has its own beauty. Part of coming to terms with the aging body is realizing how precious life is. To focus on lines and wrinkles is a waste of time; it's just life taking its course.

Zausner Richard, what has been the impact of your art in writing the book, *The Art of Aging*?

Richard Matzkin For us these art projects were very important and generated thoughts for the book. It just came about as a natural expression from our art. We'd like to pass on some of the things we've learned to the baby boomers because it is an important time for them. We want people to read the book, see the art, and get from it some of what we've gotten. It's a gift. The whole of our life is our work of art whether we use paint or clay as a medium of expression. Our real art is how we live day to day. It's how we live with integrity, how much of ourselves we give to our work, to the people we love, and to our world.

Zausner Are you working on a new project now?

Alice Matzkin Yes, we are working on a traveling exhibit to museums around the country to expose the highs and lows of aging.

This interview with Alice and Richard Matzkin originally appeared on April 30, 2013 at *http://agingandcreativity.blogspot.com/2013/04/alice-richard-matzkin.html.*

Nelson Shanks
Realist Painting with Humanistic Depth

Nelson is an extraordinary realist painter whose collections are cherished all over the world. He has generously shared his skills and interest with others by founding Studio Incamminati in Philadelphia to teach the rigors of realist painting.

Photo © Annalisa Shanks

Zausner Your sensitivity and inclination to art showed itself in your early childhood years: "I started painting when I was five." Did your parents encourage your passion for art? Were they creative individuals?

Shanks My mother was a pianist, so I was listening to great music all day long as a child and even now. And my father left for World War II, and in preparation for coming back, he bought an oil painting set for himself. I, at age five, promptly used it up.

And so, I would have been five when I did the first oil painting. Maybe not exactly what the average child would do because I was very interested in space and light and shadow and a few other things.

He also bought my mother one of the better coffee table books of that time; of course, they're nothing like the ones now. It had illustrations of some of the great artists from the Early Renaissance on through the Impressionist, maybe even Post-Impressionist. It was about an inch-thick book, and I pretty much wore it out—just fascinated by the paintings. My favorites were, at that time, a certain early Renoir and then Rembrandt and Ingres and art like that. Even at age five, I was captivated by this book and by art.

Zausner When you were using that oil painting kit, were you looking at pictures at that time—or in the mirror—or at your mother?

Shanks Actually at 5 years old, needless to say, I had no experience. I had no formal education, no education at all.

And my aunt, who I think was working in Los Alamos on the nuclear projects, couldn't send any postcards from there, so she sent things from Albuquerque, New Mexico. And so I received this Albuquerque postcard—I didn't, my family did—and it was an Indian adobe house with these poles sticking out of the front and cast shadows running down the front of the adobe. And I found that fascinating, and that's what I painted—not normally what, as they say, a 5year old would paint. We still have that silly little picture.

As far as encouragement is concerned, I don't think I received any negative response. But my parents certainly were not cheerleaders, so it was something sort of in between. I would run to my parents every five minutes and say, "Look, look. This is the best thing I've ever done." They didn't ridicule me at least.

Zausner Your father must have particularly had some art sensitivity. How many fathers from World War II, having been away, or not even away, would buy an oil painting set and this particular book?

Shanks True, he had even done a pastel or two. Although he was a very busy businessman, he did have interest there.

Zausner As a teenager you demonstrated not just incredible talent but also a strong sense of independence. You began studying at the Art Students League in NYC at eighteen and managed to earn your own tuition through work at the school. Do you ever look back and wonder about being so young with such drive and focus?

Shanks It is kind of remarkable; I honestly can't

account for it. I did go to college for a couple of years and I was thoroughly bored. I would find myself on weekends running to museums and studying various paintings, particularly among which was Rembrandt, of course. By the time I got to New York, I was completely captivated by the idea of being a painter, and so I dedicated my whole life to it. Beginning then work was something I enjoyed. Work—if painting is work—why, then I was working. But I feel a little guilty calling it "work" because I am so involved in it. It's a compulsion, and it's gratifying at the same time—very gratifying.

Zausner With prestigious grants you studied in Italy, returning later to teach in Memphis, Chicago, New York (Art Students League, The National Academy of Design), and then Bucks County, Pennsylvania. During the years that you were strengthening your skills as a realist painter, were you also reflecting on your next move to art education?

Shanks Quite frankly, at that point, I was consumed with learning all these skills myself and gaining capability. I was aware that it was just completely incredulous that the teaching level was so pathetic that I just felt challenged to try to do something about it in my own way. And I've had a compulsion to do that ever since, for the last fifty years.

Zausner You have continued to teach. You generously established an art apprentice program in your home studio at no cost to the student and then considering the high demand for developing skills in painting realism, you founded Studio Incamminati in Philadelphia. That was a huge investment of your time and energy. What support did you have to make that happen so successfully?

Shanks Well, the students who came to me pleading that I teach in Philadelphia were my biggest, let's say, fan club, and they were the most encouraging because they were very, very excited about the idea of something being created. The first few years, I was the sole teacher, and so I was there teaching two or three days a week, all day. And it was sort of holding back my own work. So, as the years have gone by, I've had students whom I have trained become the teachers. And this is part of the philosophy—the students become teachers and start doing a little bit of teaching rather early on in their education. Now we've developed some absolutely superb teachers and painters who are going around this country and the world teaching. This is only the beginning of what will definitely be expanded.

Zausner That's sensational. It's really giving back.

Shanks It's working big time.

Zausner Your portraits are rich in realistic life details and also carry a depth of soulfulness. Who was your first well-known commissioned portrait? How did you receive that project?

Shanks Oh wow, I can barely remember. I know that a businessman, an associate of my father's, asked me to paint a portrait, but it was way too early. I didn't have that kind of confidence when I was about nineteen. Then when I was in New York studying, I was asked to paint the head minister of the All Saints Unitarian Church on Madison Avenue in New York, and I painted Dr. Walter Donald Crane. Right about that time, I also went to Europe—to Italy for a couple of years—so I painted a lot of friends and a lot of things but not high profile commissions. So let's see, oh gosh, it's very hard to remember. It's just been a question of slowly going up a staircase. And it's hard to know if there's any one point where the light starts flashing and suddenly, oh boy, I'm painting some important people. I don't put that much into the celebrity status, because I've come to the conclusion that all people have depth, and all people have something that I would love to extrude and put into a painting. And so, it's not just kings and queens and princesses that I go into with depth. It's virtually everything I paint, frankly.

Then again getting to know these people—some, I have become very good friends with. Perhaps the deepest relationship might be with Diana, but I also had a wonderful relationship with Margaret Thatcher. I painted her twice, so I spent many, many hours with her—both during the paintings and other times. We were great friends.

Generally speaking, we make friends. And because I'm painting friends, their humanity is very much in the forefront. It's very gratifying that way because I don't hide what I'm doing and then sort of flash it to them at the end. They are part of the process, and they see what I'm doing the whole way. And I think they really, really gain from it. People I never would have expected would get excited and interested in the project do become interested and excited about the project. So, that's very gratifying. I'm not just painting an object. So, it makes a big difference.

Zausner Now that you are famous and in museums, galleries, and collections all over the world, do you have an agent for your art or do commissions come to you directly?

Shanks Well, they normally come to me directly. I run across so many people, and so many people are aware of my work that I don't need someone out there peddling it. But often I'll get, for example, a recommendation—someone will be sent to me by a museum director or museum curators or people that are in the art world or that kind of thing—or just because of connections that have somehow or other been attained over the last half-century. But selling paintings—I just run across people that really want them, and that's very gratifying. Occasionally, I will have a show with an exhibition. For example I just had two very, very important exhibitions in Russia. I was invited by the Russian Academy of Art to have a major exhibition there, and I did, two years ago. And then the State Russian Museum in St. Petersburg wanted the same show and got it. So, I showed at the two very major Russian museums. And that was, I guess, word of mouth, people heard about me, or whatever, and they approached me.

Zausner You have said that "you cannot make a major difference doing things in a minor way." Has that belief driven you to succeed?

Shanks With the major things in my life, my painting, and therefore my teaching—and, of course, my family—there is no element of complacency as I approach these things, and that might be represented by calling it in a minor way. So for example—the teaching—I could teach a few students or have a few apprentices here living with me around the house, but actually I think reaching a greater number of people and influencing art worldwide is my ambition. I think we're well on the road. I think art needs some major changes. And what they call modern art is just ridiculous. I think it's time to reset the clock and reset the direction of art, and we're doing that. But it's a big responsibility to teach people not just to talk about it.

Words almost become meaningless. But I think we can change some things, but there has to be better art out there for people to grasp on to. And with great hope and luck, some of these students and I will provide that. So that's what I mean by doing something in a big way. But I don't mean that you should make—when you fix breakfast—spend a lifetime on it. I think you do have to select the most important things to address your time with.

Zausner At 75, you remain very active by painting almost daily and continuing to teach at Studio Incamminati. Do you have daily routines? Do you still have any unfulfilled goals?

Shanks I have exactly the same routine I think I've always had, but maybe it's more of a routine than it ever was. I get up early, often it's dark and I'll come to the studio very early in the morning, and I will paint without sitting down often for ten or eleven or even twelve hours.

And, it's no more difficult for me to do that now, in fact perhaps easier than it ever was because it's become quite a habit. I do know that many of my students fall on the floor in exhaustion after about an hour, and I'm like the little battery that keeps on going. And I feel I have every bit as much energy and a whole lot more experience and ability than I had when I was much younger.

Zausner Do you work out? Do you do some physical exercises that help you maintain this incredible routine?

Shanks A little, but I have little, little ambition to become an Arnold Schwarzenegger.

Zausner Do you possibly have any unfulfilled goals at this point?

Shanks Just more and better paintings—I think my paintings are almost becoming more ambitious in the last five or six years than they've ever been—and more complicated. I think they're more competent. I think they have greater appeal visually, and I think they're more exciting. I think they have greater depth, and so this is all an accumulation of knowledge that I've gained over all these years. And I'm enjoying the heck out of being competent.

But, there is nothing like knowledge, and one of my statements that I would make, unsolicited from you, is that "show me somebody that is self-taught, and I'll show you someone who is incompetent and ignorant." Because there is such a vast, vast, vast resource in art history, and those paintings and painters that have come before, that somebody who has not seen those—because if they've seen those at all and studied them at all, then they're not self-taught—they're getting it from—self-taught means total ignorance, and I'm not for that at all. I think the more you know, the greater the creativity.

This interview with Nelson Shanks originally appeared on October 12, 2013 at *http://agingandcreativity.blogspot.com/2013/10/an-interview-with-nelson-shanks.html.*

Isaiah Zagar
Mosaic Muralist:
"Mirror, Mirror on the Wall…"

Photo © Judith Zausner

Isaiah's Peace Corps roots and his art training at Pratt Institute are the subtle influences of his citywide mosaic murals in Philadelphia. His most famous project, Magic Gardens, *is a mosaic space created with broken mirrors and other recycled elements that surface walls and floors and are indeed magical.*

Zausner I've learned that your first creative awareness, perhaps explosion, was when you were 3 years old. You were taught to color within lines in your coloring book but then promptly took the crayon off the page, to move it along the table, wall, and refrigerator. So from a primary lesson on boundaries you immediately pushed outside the boundaries. Perhaps this was your first mural of memory?

Zagar I don't even know if I would consider that a mural. Just feeling the textures of everything and being excited by the visual quality that was presented and that it was different than what was there already. It changed the paradigm and changed the way things looked. Could you call it a mural? I don't think you could call it a mural. You could call it a place where empty spaces were filled with ideas and rituals. But in my case it was just a child scribbling, a graffiti process, a naming that said, "I'm here... I'm doing this thing." And, of course, it changed everything. And, of course, my mother flipped out; she was appalled at what I had done and that was a fantastic eye-opener for me. I saw the amazing changes that went on in her from seeing what I had done.

You can't call it art but it was a creative experience. It was to color, what I call total embellishment, the continuing and continuing without borders. It was a moment in time that was very powerful to me and continues to resonate. I have very strong visual memories of the actual event.

Zausner After graduating from Pratt Institute and subsequently working as a Peace Corps Craft Developer, you had a personal crisis. You had a nervous breakdown and tried to commit suicide. Yet you turned this around when you began putting discards on the wall with cement and began your mural art. It is ironic that you have rescued these broken bits of mirrors ("My favorite material to use is mirrors because mirrors reflect the present") and pottery, which began with your wife's imported pottery and Eyes Gallery retail store, and elevated them to a new status and purpose just as the process of doing so brought you out of your mental health problems. Do you have thoughts on this?

Zagar I wasn't broken a bit. I was broken a lot. Your description of it is very clear. I don't know what more I can add.

I was given a scholarship to take a class with Emanuel Bromberg, an artist and a painter. He saw something in my work and took me to visit the work of Clarence Schmidt.

Clarence Schmidt was an artist who was not an artist; he was a man who just created with discards. I was brought to see the folk art environment or the vernacular environment of Clarence Schmidt, and it knocked me for a loop, my heart began to beat very rapidly. The way I tell the story—there were no young women around, so what does a 19 year old man say about his heart palpitating so fast at seeing something that was outrageous and different from anything that I had ever seen? I just wanted to be there for a while. I immediately climbed the fence, and I went inside the structure, and I was just knocked out by its insanity, its absolute insanity of what I had known to be art. In fact I couldn't even call it art—I didn't call it art—I was just knocked out.

After the nervous breakdown, I had to rebuild myself as an artist. How could I be an artist after a nervous breakdown? That was in 1969 and I was 28 years old. I needed to find a place where I could be a Clarence, not worried about the marketplace, but living the life of the artist. I needed to find something so devastated that I can build it up from scratch and that became South Street (Philadelphia).

I only wanted to create art. I didn't want to deal with the real world. I created a fantasy world—an art object that I created à la Clarence Schmidt with the same kind of impetus—using found objects, derelict materials, free materials, materials that I scavenged the world over.

Last year over 60,000 people visited Magic Gardens and more have traveled through the city to see the other mosaic murals.

Zausner Your flagship mural, *Magic Gardens* on South Street in Philadelphia, is an extraordinary and large assemblage of many broken and recycled elements plus your own poetic and artful expressions ("I built this sanctuary to be inhabited by my ideas and my fantasies"). How do you maintain it?

Does the weather impact it?

Zagar Yes, the weather does majorly impact it. The piece changes rapidly from year to year. It has intrinsic in it a death knoll, and whether we can stave off the death knoll forever is not clear because I was not and am not a structural engineer. I worked with intuition and worked without much regard to the longevity of the project, always thinking that it was like abstract expressionism—that I could keep changing it, that it was ever changing. A project that could be continually reinvented, not only by myself, but also by other people. That it could be kept moving and changing rather than a piece of art that was static. I'm not sure about that anymore, whether the soul of it can remain intact with so many other hands involved in it.

Zausner Your art gives purpose to the recycled movement. As an honorary Dumpster Diver, you have inspired artists and aspiring artists to view trashed objects in a different way. Though you don't go in the dumpsters yourself, your network of dumpster diver donors keep you actively sourced. How do you store all of these pieces until they are used?

Zagar Well, I have a garage here that is useful, and I have a big building in South Philadelphia that I have been working on for the past seven years, and it is a useful place to store a lot. I've also run out of the energy to do reconnaissance missions to get materials. I have essentially slowed down to a non-work stop, basically because I have so much that I have done.

I thought that I was skirting the problems of storing art, because I was making the art in the street, and when I was doing paintings on canvas, I didn't use stretch bars so that I could roll them up, or I was even doing paintings on rice paper. That was as easy as pie. I would paint a big painting with several pieces of paper, and I could roll it up and store. However, no one was seeing any of these things. They were made and stored, and even I didn't look at some of them again. I was having this tremendous problem—although I didn't know it—of overproducing.

The amount of work I have done is staggering. I was able to give one of the larger pieces to the Philadelphia Museum of Art because it related to Anne d'Harnoncourt. I made this piece called *The Futurist* because she was very involved in a show of the futurists. I made a big 10 x 12 feet mosaic that was accepted by the PMA as a gift. I thought this would be the beginning of the possibility of moving these big panel mosaics, some as big as the wall.

Zausner And your work is all about exploring boundaries on different levels. In creating mosaic murals, you use lots of broken mirrors and glass; those pieces have changed from their original state to one with broken boundaries. Then these pieces are placed in assemblage to create a mural where the boundaries merge and disappear with other elements, and they radically challenge conceptions of what a building wall should look like. Do you consciously explore boundaries in making art?

Zagar Well, the art that I make in the City on Walls have boundaries now. They actually didn't have boundaries when I was able to do complete walls, the complete building, then I never thought about boundaries, in fact. In this case, where we are sitting in my studio, any place where I looked out onto where I had control over I embellished, and they didn't have rectangular boundaries. But when I do the murals in the City or on panels, they do have boundaries, and they do have themes.

I just finished one for a fitness center on Reed Street (between 7th & 8th) and it's a long mural—about 200 feet long by 7 feet high and it has its boundaries. It doesn't go all the way up through the building, just has its boundaries on one level. Although it has figures that begin at the feet sometimes and only end at the middle of their bodies. You can imagine that it could go to the next level.

Magic Gardens is in the center of a big city, and it's on a street that is known for its idiosyncrasy, its movement of hippies and how they changed the way people looked at things. It has an identity that people want to see before they even know about Philadelphia's *Magic Gardens*. They want to come to the street so they do happen upon the garden, and if it was in some outlying area that didn't have that reputation, then it wouldn't have the power that it has—the environment, the placement of an art object is so important.

Zausner You have completed over 130 outdoor murals and, in doing that, covered more than 50,000 square feet of Philadelphia. This is an enormous art legacy. Now at 74, have you scaled your art to less physical installations? What's on your horizon?

Zagar I've just completed small pieces for a show of small pieces but I'm not enamored of the challenges of small pieces.

I don't know what the future will bring at all. I have rebounded several times from complete breakdown failures (mental that pushed into the physical). Now I'm in another one; I'm not whole yet, and I don't know if I can get whole. So I can't prognosticate about the future without the feelings of the present. That is how one thinks about the future.

Author's note: In a subsequent follow up to this inter-view, Isaiah offered the following additional remarks on the above question:

In this past year, I successfully completed two large-scale projects in Mexico. At the same time, I experienced a personal change. Fortunately, I am transformed and have come out whole on the other side with wellness and with gratitude to new medication. I had to let go and reach for mental renewal. As we get older, it is especially important to flex and change and as Buddha says, "Everything changes, nothing remains without change." And so I remind myself often of that and try to bend toward a more optimistic way of thinking.

This interview with Isaiah Zagar originally appeared on December 30, 2013 at *http://agingandcreativity.blogspot.com/2013/12/an-interview-with-isaiah-zagar-mosaic.html.*

Tobi Zausner
Artist, Psychologist, Writer

Tobi is an extraordinary painter as well as a research psychologist and psychotherapist. Her book, When Walls Become Doorways: Creativity and the Transforming Illness, *is a testament to the power of creativity during a health crisis.*

Judith Zausner Tobi, you began making art at a very young age. Do you remember some of your first experiences? Your first paintings?

Tobi Zausner I began making art in earnest when I was about three and a half years old. I don't remember the pieces of art I produced but what I do remember is the process, the thrill of focusing on something and watching it change before my eyes. Each piece of art was its own world that would emerge as I created it. This wonderful feeling has stayed with me today.

Judith Zausner Often exceptional talent generates acclaim. What awards, prizes, and other notable distinctions have you received for your art? Which accolades are particularly special to you and why?

Tobi Zausner Like many people, I have won prizes, but I think the greatest prize is within. It is the feeling of accomplishment that comes with creating a work of art or writing an article on psychology that I believe communicates its message to others and comes up to a standard that gives me joy. We are all capable of doing something that brings us great satisfaction, and this happiness with accomplishment is a prize available to everyone.

Judith Zausner Over the years as an artist, and then as a psychologist, you became interested in artists who continued to be creative despite difficult obstacles. In your book, *When Walls Become Doorways: Creativity and the Transforming Illness*, you profile many of these amazing artists. Can you talk about your personal impetus for writing this book and the value for everyone?

Tobi Zausner The impetus for writing *When Walls Become Doorways* was my personal experience with major illnesses that became turning points in my life. When I was diagnosed with ovarian cancer in 1989, my doctor did not expect me to survive, but

I did and my life transformed. After this illness, in addition to being an artist, I also became a psychologist. In the 1970s I was sick for seven years as a result of being poisoned by an insecticide. Yet it was during this period that my mature style of painting emerged, and I began to show my work professionally. Having had this happen to me, I became sensitive to the same dynamic in others. In *When Walls Become Doorways* I feature artists, who have vision problems, hearing loss, cancer, neurological illnesses, and disabling accidents among other conditions, yet all of these artists transformed their work and their lives. What is initially viewed as a tragedy can instead become an opportunity.

Judith Zausner You became involved in psychology research in graduate school and then received a doctorate combining art and psychology. How did this happen and what are you investigating?

Tobi Zausner I actually believe I got a doctorate by accident because I had no concept of getting a PhD when I started graduate school. My intended goal was to get a Masters in art. Then I started taking classes in the psychology department, and a whole new way of thinking became available. One course, in particular, on the psychology of art, changed my life and defined my path by combining psychology and art. My work in psychology focuses on the creative process. I have investigated how creativity can be used as a tool for resilience, helping us to bounce back from difficulties, and now I am researching the altered states of consciousness that can occur during times of creativity. These states are not related to any drugs, but occur as part of the rapture of creating something new.

Judith Zausner To be dedicated as an artist and as a psychologist is very demanding life work. How do you balance that?

Tobi Zausner Art and psychology balance each other and in doing so they balance me. I have always had a very demanding life, and work is the fire that runs through my veins. It is a life force, and it is a road that I can never really predict no matter how hard I try. So in response I just keep going.

Judith Zausner Now at 70, what are your expectations, visions, dreams?

Tobi Zausner I want to keep working. Artists die with their boots on, and I also have no plans to retire as a psychologist. About expectations—we can expect what we want, but what we most often receive is the unexpected, and this unexpected result, this unplanned for harvest, this undreamt of situation, is often greater, more interesting, more challenging, and more transformational than having one's previously intended plans and dreams come true. It is the dreams you didn't realize you could dream that take you down paths you never imagined you would be able to travel.

This interview with my sister Tobi Zausner original-ly appeared on July 28, 2013 at *http://agingandcre-ativity.blogspot.com/2013/07/tobi-zausner-extraor-dinary-painter.html.*

GALLERY

William Daley

Vesica One

Cyclops

Joshua's Cistern

Nelson Shanks

Goats, Oil on Canvas 24" x 20¼" Unframed 2014

Houdon and Coins,
Oil on Canvas 34" x 20" Unframed 2014

Portrait if His Holiness, John Paul II,
Oil on Canvas 54" x 50" Unframed 2002

Tobi Zausner

Quanah

Travelogues

Wind on the Lake

Richard Blake

Frederick Douglass

Martin Luther King, Jr.

Woman in Folding Chair

Barbara Hanselman

Paisleaf Pendant Reversible Necklace

Pillow Box

Cat Come Home Rattle

Betsy Hershberg

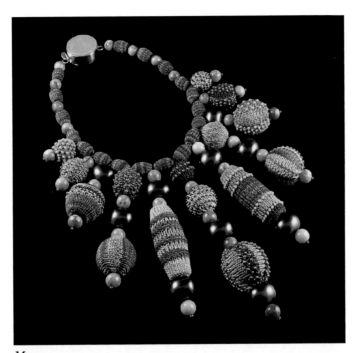

Myra

Uni II

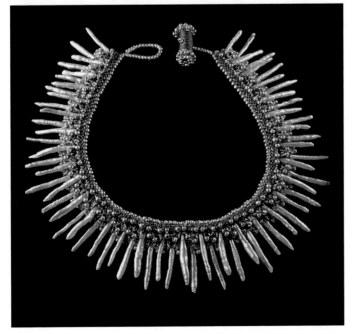

Pearlburst

Ed Bing Lee

Delectable

Delectable

Delectable

Yvone Bobrowicz

Cosmic Series

Cosmic Series

Floorscape

Mitch Lyons

Blue Shadow

Russell's Farm

Judith Leiber

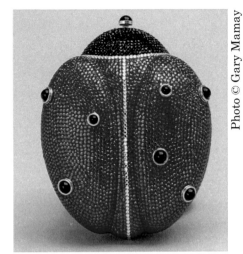

Ladybug Minaudiere

Buddha Minaudiere

Butterfly Minaudiere

Richard Matzkin

Fear of Alzheimer's

Lovers

Left

Alice Matzkin

Beatrice at 105, Women of Age

Phyllis, Naked Truth

Aunt Kitty, Declining Years

Isaiah Zagar

Magic Gardens, Philadelphia

Kaffe Fassett

Endnotes

IMAGINATION, CREATIVITY, AND CONFIDENCE

1 Querna, Betsy, "Paul McCartney and 'Yesterday'," U.S. News & World Report, accessed July 18, 2010, http://health.usnews.com/usnews/health/articles/060515/15dreams.b3.htm.

CREATIVE THINKING AND POSITIVE AGING

2 Dean, Jeremy, "Aging and the Positivity Effect," PsyBlog, accessed July 31, 2011, http://www.spring.org.uk/2007/07/ageing-and-positivity-effect.php.

CELEBRATING YOUR LEGACY

3 Civic Ventures, accessed December 19, 2009, http://www.civicventures.org

4 "Stories," Civic Ventures, accessed December 19, 2009, http://www.civicventures.org/stories.cfm. .

5 Weber, Bruce, "Gene D. Cohen, Geriatric Psychiatrist, Dies at 65," The New York Times, accessed December 19, 2009, http://www.nytimes.com/2009/11/12/us/12cohen.html

6 "Meet Our Founder: Alexandra Scott," Alex's Lemonade Stand Foundation, accessed December 19, 2009, http://www.alexslemonade.org/about/meet-alex.

7 Hudson, Claudia, "Community Hero: J.A. and Geraldine Reynolds," My Hero, accessed December 19, 2009, http://www.myhero.com/go/hero.asp?hero=Bruce_Garden_Sept11.

8 Dress for Success, accessed December 19, 2009, http://dressforsuccess.org/.

HOPE, CREATIVITY, AND CHANGE
9 Canfield, Clarke, "Maine Artist Creates HOPE Image Decades after LOVE," USA Today, accessed November 17, 2008, http://www.usatoday.com/news/topstories/2008-08-30-2854729396_x.htm?loc=interstitialskip.
10 "Barack Obama Victory – Obama Wins – Music Video – Hope & Change – Yes We Can!!!," YouTube, accessed November 17, 2008, http://www.youtube.com/watch?v=SBsukHYSpqo.
11 Cast Coverz!, accessed November 17, 2008, http://www.castcoverz.com/designer-color-crutches-crutch-covers.php.

AM I AN ARTIST?
12 Gardiner, Li, "10 Points of Light," Artistresource.org, accessed September 23, 2010, http://www.artistresource.org/artlife.htm#10pointsoflight.
13 "Above Ground: Information on Artists III: NYC Aging Artists (2008)," The Research Center for Arts and Culture, accessed September 23, 2010, http://artsandcultureresearch.org/research/above-ground/.
14 "When Walls Become Doorways: Creativity and the Transforming Illness," Tobi Zausner, accessed September 23, 2010, http://www.tobizausner.com/9_WWD_P.html.

HAPPINESS, CREATIVITY, AND THE OLDER ADULT
15 Gilbert, Dan, "The Surprising Science of Happiness," TED talk, accessed January 13, 2011, http://www.ted.com/talks/dan_gilbert_asks_why_are_we_happy.html.

16 Minkel, J.R., "Happiness: Good for Creativity, Bad for Single-Minded Focus," Scientific American, accessed January 13, 2011, http://www.scientificamerican.com/article.cfm?id=happiness-good-for-creati.

17 Matthiesen, Susanne, "Rekindling the Creative Spark as You Age," Newsweek, accessed January 13, 2011, http://www.newsweekshowcase.com/retirement/articles/rekindling-the-creative.

18 Aging Artfully, accessed January 13, 2011, http://www.agingartfully.com/.

CREATIVITY, CONFORMITY, AND AGING

19 "The Barbie Story – Interview with Ruth Handler and Elliot Handler, Mattel Co-Founders," YouTube video, 2:38, posted by "BFC Spotlight," February 15, 2013, https://www.youtube.com/watch?v=dj0hpSP-TEw&spfreload=10.

20 Dean, Jeremy, "Why Group Norms Kill Creativity," PsyBlog, accessed March 14, 2010, http://www.spring.org.uk/2009/06/why-group-norms-kill-creativity.php.

21 Maisel, Eric, The Meaning Solution: Create Purpose, Power & Passion, accessed March 14, 2010, http://meaningsolution.com/discount?a_aid=4b993aa60a2f4&a_bid=55c9b.

INSPIRED CREATIVITY

22 Further biographical information is available at http://en.wikipedia.org/wiki/Hugh_Herr.

23 Further biographical information is available at http://en.wikipedia.org/wiki/Aimee_Mullins.

24 Amy Purdy's blog can accessed at http://amy-purdy.blogspot.com.

25 An interview by CNN's Anderson Cooper can be accessed at http://ac360.blogs.cnn.com/category/adrianne-haslet-davis/

26 Mike Schultz's website can be accessed at http://www.monstermikeschultz.com.

27 Tozer, James, "Former Soldier Who Lost Both Legs in Afghanistan Fitted with World's Most Advanced Bionic Know Worth £70,000 which Works with Wii Gaming Technology," Daily Mail, accessed February 28, 2014, http://www.dailymail.co.uk/health/article-2557465/Former-soldier-lost-legs-Afghanistan-fitted-worlds-advanced-bionic-knee-worth-70-000-works-Wii-gaming-technology.html.

28 Additonal biographical information is available at http://www.media.mit.edu/people/hherr.

29 Mullins, Aimee, "My 12 Pairs of Legs," Ted video, 9:58, posted February, 2009, http://www.ted.com/talks/aimee_mullins_prosthetic_aesthetics.

30 "Boston Bombing Survivor's Emotional Journey," YouTube video, 7:52, CNN, October 18, 2013, https://www.youtube.com/watch?v=YzHsfQ8nWkQ.

31 "Dancing with the Stars – Amy Purdy & Derek Hough's Contemporary (Week 3), YouTube video, 1:26, posted by ABC Television Network, April 1, 2014, https://www.youtube.com/watch?v=IMSP5hIz8pU.

32 Dutton, Judy, "Extreme Sports Star Mike Schultz Built Himself a New Limb," Wired, accessed February 28, 2014, http://www.wired.com/2013/01/man-of-steel/.

THE EVOLVING WHEELCHAIR: INNOVATION, ADAPTABILITY, AND DESIGN

33 "35 Wildly Wonderful Wheelchair Design Concepts," Love These Pics, accessed February 28, 2013, *http://www.lovethesepics.com/2012/09/35-wildly-wonderful-wheelchair-design-concepts/.*

34 "Disability Arts Online," Freewheeling, accessed February 28, 2013, http://www.wearefreewheeling.org.uk/.

35 "Carrier Robotic Wheelchair," Vimeo video, 1:24, posted by Bilge Demirci, 2008, http://vimeo.com/40515866.

OCTOGENARIANS CREATE FASHION HISTORY

36 A description of Richard Press's Bill Cunningham New York is available at http://www.zeitgeistfilms.com/billcunninghamnewyork/.

37 "Roberto Capucci: Art into Fashion," Philadelphia Museum of Art, accessed April 5, 2011, http://www.philamuseum.org/exhibitions/411.html.

38 Additional information on The Leiber Collection is available from http://www.leibermuseum.org.

APFEL AT AGE 90:
MORE IS MORE AND LESS IS SIMPLY LESS

39 Iris Apfel's biography can be read at http://en.wikipedia.org/wiki/Iris_Apfel.

REINVENTING EMBROIDERY:
EXPERIMENTAL AND EXTRAORDINARY ART

40 Poetics of Form, Synderman-Works Galleries, accessed March 31, 2012, http://www.snyderman-works.com/news/shizuko-kimura-the-poetics-of-form-opens-at-moore.

41 A selection of Reichek's art can be viewed at http://elainereichek.com/Images.htm.

42 Daniel Kornrumpf's portfolio and resume is available on his website at http://danielkornrumpf.com/home.html.

43 Clyde Olliver's blog can be found at http://clydeolliver.wordpress.com.

44 Laura Splan's professional projects can be viewed at http://www.laurasplan.com/.

45 Examples of Christa Maiwald's embroidered portraits are available at http://www.christamaiwald.com/.

CELEBRATING CREATIVE CENTENARIANS

46 Bernstein, Rachel, "Longevity—It's in your Genes," Los Angeles Times, accessed November 11, 2010, http://

articles.latimes.com/2010/jul/02/science/la-sci-longevity-genes-20100702.

47 Additional biographical information is available at http://en.wikipedia.org/wiki/Irving_Kahn.

48 Additional biographical information is available at http://en.wikipedia.org/wiki/Rita_Levi-Montalcini

49 Kuchment, Anna, "Elliott Carter, Still Composing at 100," Newsweek, accessed on November 11, 2010, http://www.newsweek.com/elliott-carter-still-composing-100-83269.

50 Additional biographical information is available at http://en.wikipedia.org/wiki/Eva_Zeisel.

51 Sulzberger, A.G., "At 103, A Judge has One Caveat: No Lengthy Trials," The New York Times, accessed November 11, 2010, http://www.nytimes.com/2010/09/17/us/17judge.html?_r=1&emc=eta1.

52 Additional biographical information is available at http://en.wikipedia.org/wiki/Milton_Rogovin.

53 Additional biographical information is available at https://www.youtube.com/watch?v=QlccsLr48Mw.

54 Additional biographical information is available at http://en.wikipedia.org/wiki/Malcolm_Renfrew.

55 NPR's All Things Considered featured a story on Corwin, which can be accessed at http://www.npr.org/templates/story/story.php?storyId=126414628.

56 An in-depth profile on Barnett can be read at http://www.nytimes.com/2010/10/27/nyregion/27artist.html.

57 Further information on Gruber's life story, Ahead of Time, is available at http://ruthgruberthemovie.com.

REUSE, REPURPOSE, RECREATE

58 Preuss, Simone, "Seven Pieces of Furniture Made of Old Bicycles," 1800recycling.com. accessed June 30, 2012, http://www.1800recycling.com/2010/11/creative-furniture-items-bike-parts/.

59 Pyke, Kristy, "Intermission: A Coffee Shop Made Out of Shipping Crates," Good, accessed June 30, 2012, http://www.good.is/post/intermission-a-coffee-shop-made-out-of-shipping-crates/.

60 Stankorb, Sarah, "Upcycling's Upshot: How Urban Mushroom Farmers Turned Scavenging into a Business," Good, accessed June 30, 2012, http://www.good.is./post/upcycling-s-upshot-how-urban-mushroom-farmers-turned-scavening-into-a-business/.

61 McMurray, Cathy, "Dazzling Chandaliers Made from Discarded Objects," Habit of Art, accessed June 30, 2012, http://www.habit-of-art.blogspot.com/2011/06/dazzling-chandaliers-made-from.html.

62 The Louise Nevelson Foundation offers numerous resources for further study of Nevelson's work. See http://www.louisenevelsonfoundation.org/resources.php.

63 Additional biographical information is available at http://www.artarchive.com/artarchive/C/cornell.html.

64 Additional biographical information is available at http://www.theartstory.org/artist-chamberlain-john.htm.

65 McMurray, Cathy, "Transforming Ordinary Objects into Incredible Works of Art," Habit of Art, accessed June 30, 2012, http://www.habit-of-art.blogspot.com/2011/01/transforming-ordinary-objects-into.html.

66 Petru, Alexis, "Amazing Sculptures Made from Ocean Litter," Earth911.com, accessed June 30, 2012, http://earth911.com/news/2012/04/13/washed-ashore-sculptures-made-from-ocean-litter/?utm_source=Earth911.com+Weekly+Newsletter&utm_campaign=2fc4cb395a-_8_Kickstart_Ocean_Trash_Sculptures6_22_2012&utm_medium=email.

CHALLENGING ART

67 Additional biographical information is available at http://en.wikipedia.org/wiki/James_Charles_Castle.

68 Additional biographical information is at http://en.wikipedia.org/wiki/Georgia_O%27Keeffe

69 The Mouth and Foot Painting Artists website can be accessed at http://www.mfpa.co.uk.

70 Further information about Tim Lefens is available at http://www.philia.ca/cms_en/page1350.cfm.

71 A.R.T. can be accessed online at http://www.artrealization.org.

72 Additional biographical information is available at http://en.wikipedia.org/wiki/Frida_Kahlo.

73 Judith Scott's website is available at http://www.hidden-worlds.com/judithscott/.

ACCESSIBILITY OF VISUAL ART

74 The National Endowment for the Arts offers an extensive resource guide at http://arts.endow.gov/resources/accessibility/Planning/VisualArts.pdf.

75 The National Arts and Disability Center's website is available at http://nadc.ucla.edu/.

76 The MoMA's Alzheimer Project can be accessed at http://www.moma.org/meetme/.

77 Further information about Metropolitan Museum of Art's "Discoveries" program is available at http://www.metmuseum.org/events/pdf/Discoveries2007_2008.pdf.

78 Further information about the Philadelphia Museum of Art's work on accessibility is available at http://www.philamuseum.org/visit/56-282-88.html.

79 Further program information is available at http://www.philamuseum.org/visit/56-282-309-93.html.

THE VALUE OF ARTS & CRAFTS

80 A "Founder's Tribute" to Dr. Cohen can be accessed at http://www.gwumc.edu/cahh/founder.html.

81 Information about Jefferson-Myrna Brind Center of Integrative Medicine is available at http://www.bravewell.org/current_projects/clinical_network/jefferson_myrna_brind_center/.

82 Root-Bernstein, Michele and Robert, "Arts and Crafts: Keys to Scientific Creativity," Psychology Today, accessed October 19, 2009, http://www.psychologytoday.com/blog/imagine/200903/arts-and-crafts-keys-scientific-creativity.

WHEN WALLS BECOME DOORWAYS

83 Tobi Zausner's professional website is available at http://www.tobizausner.com/9_WWD_P.html.

Made in the USA
Middletown, DE
24 May 2015